Introduction to Programmable Logic Controllers

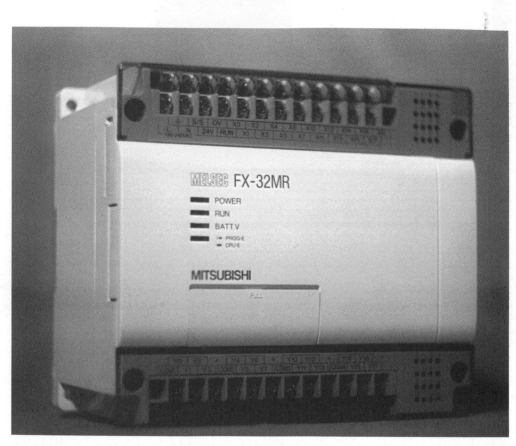

Mitsubishi FX PLC type 32 MR

Introduction to Programmable Logic Controllers

The Mitsubishi FX

J E Ridley Diploma in Electrical Engineering, C.Eng, M.I.E.E.

Senior Lecturer
Worcester College of Technology

and

Visiting Lecturer
Mitsubishi Electric (UK) Ltd
Hatfield

A member of the Hodder Headline Group
LONDON • SYDNEY • AUCKLAND
Copublished in North, Central and South America by
John Wiley & Sons, Inc., New York • Toronto

First published in Great Britain in 1997 by
Arnold, a member of the Hodder Headline Group
338 Euston Road, London NW1 3BH

Copublished in North, Central and South America by
John Wiley & Sons, Inc., 605 Third Avenue,
New York, NY 10158-0012

Whilst the advice and information in this book is believed to be true and
accurate at the date of going to press, neither the author[s] nor the publisher
can accept any legal responsibility or liability for any errors or omissions
that may be made.

British Library Cataloguing in Publication Data
A catalogue record for this book is available from the British Library

Library of Congress Cataloging-in-Publication Data
A catalog record for this book is available from the Library of Congress

ISBN 0 340 67666 3

ISBN 0 470 23729 5 (Wiley)

Typeset in 10/11pt Times by Gray Publishing, Tunbridge Wells, Kent
Printed and bound in Great Britain by J. W. Arrowsmith, Bristol

To my wife Greta.
For her help and support, without which I would never have
been able to complete this work.

Contents

Preface

This book is an introduction to programming the Mitsubishi FX range of programmable logic controllers (PLCs). It is intended for both students and engineers who wish to take the first steps into programming PLCs. In doing so, they will become aware of the wide diversity of applications for which PLCs can be used.

Students who are undertaking engineering courses will find that the text covers most of the requirements for the following BTEC units.

- Programmable Logic Controllers N 3316F
- Engineering Applications of Programmable Logic Controllers N/H 11965G

Acknowledgements

I acknowledge with grateful thanks the help I have received from Mitsubishi (UK) Ltd. and their people without whose advice and assistance this book would not have been possible.

Malcolm Robbins	Head Mitsubishi UK Customer Training Centre.
John Willingham	Assistant UK Training Manager.
Ian Christie	Formerly Midlands Sales Executive, Mitsubishi UK.

Many thanks Ian, for introducing me to the 'World of the PLC'.

Wai Cheung
David Duckworth
Roger Payne
Roy Styler

I also acknowledge with grateful thanks, the support of my colleagues and management at Worcester College of Technology and also those whom I have met whilst doing PLC Courses throughout the UK, who have unstintingly passed on 'nuggets of gold' from their practical knowledge of PLC systems: Terry Walker, Allied Bakeries, Reading; William Bevan, Allied Bakeries, Stoke on Trent; Andrew Giles, Allied Bakeries, West Bromwich; Ian McLaren, Amcor Ltd, Mold; John Pudge, Arbour Tech, Leominster; Philip Edwards, Brico Ltd, Coventry; Dennis Pearce, Caradon Mira, Cheltenham; Steve Carlin, Ceramaspeed, Droitwich; Gary Smith, CPC Foods, Redditch; Brian Mills, Ercon Ltd, Willenhall; Ilka Rudzio, Hella Ltd., Banbury; Ken Bloomfield, Holden Hydroman, Bromyard; Alan Law, Ishida UK, West Bromwich; John Ferris, Johnson Controls, Leamington Spa; Brian O' Neil, Lee and Perrins, Worcester; Jim Facey, Model Boards, Preston; Richard Faulder, Moorland Electronics, Stoke on Trent; Stuart Shaw, Powergen, Aberystwyth; Philip Townsend, Rank Xerox, Mitcheldean; John Collins, Redland Aggregates, Worksop; Marvin James, Rubery Owen Wheels, Willenhall; Eric Davies, Sarah Lee (Brylcream), Slough; Ray Eastwood, Stena Offshore, Aberdeen; Chris Mayne, Thorn Lighting, Hereford; Roy Abson, UK-NSI, Redditch; Tony Potter, United Steel, Bromsgrove; Simon Poole, Welsh Water, Swansea; Martin Lawrence, Yamasaki Machine Tools Ltd, Worcester.

1
Introduction to PLCs

The need for low-cost, versatile and easily commissioned controllers has resulted in the development of programmable logic controllers which can be used quickly and easily in a wide variety of industrial applications.

The most powerful facility which PLCs possess, is that they can be easily programmed to produce their control function, instead of having to be laboriously hardwired, as required in electromagnetic relay control systems.

The design of simple PLC ladder diagrams, that is ones that do not use advanced instructions, can still use conventional relay system techniques. Therefore, the skills of an earlier technology are still viable with those of the new.

The PLC was initially designed by General Motors in 1968, who were interested in producing a control system for their assembly plants and which did not have to be replaced every time a new model of car was manufactured.

The initial specification for the PLC was:

1. Easily programmed and reprogrammed, preferably in plant to enable its sequence of operations to be altered.
2. Easily maintained and repaired, preferably using plug-in modules.
3. (a) More reliable in a plant environment.
   (b) Smaller than its relay equivalent.
4. Cost effective in comparison with solid-state and relay systems then in use.

1.1 Comparison of PLC and RELAY systems

A comparison of these systems is shown in the table below:

Characteristic	PLC	Relay
Price per function	Low (If equivalent relay program uses more than 10 relays.)	Low
Physical size	Very compact	Bulky
Operating speed	Fast	Slow
Electrical noise immunity	Good	Excellent
Construction	Easy to program in ladder using a computer	Time consuming, wiring coils and contacts
Capable of complicated operations	Yes	No
Ease of changing the control sequence	Very simple	Very difficult
Maintenance	Excellent, PLCs rarely fail	Poor, if large number of mechanical contacts and coils have to be maintained.

1.2 PLC Software

To be able to design a PLC program using a computer, it is essential for the PLC software to have the following facilities:

1. Programs can be designed using conventional relay ladder diagram techniques.
2. Test the program is valid for use on the chosen PLC.
3. Programs can be permanently saved either on the computer's hard disk or on floppy $3^1/_2$ inch disks.
4. Programs can be reloaded from either the hard or the floppy disk.
5. Ladder diagram contacts and coils can be annotated with suitable comments.
6. Hard-copy printouts can be obtained.
7. The program can be transferred to the PLC via a serial link.
8. The program within the PLC can be transferred back to the computer.
9. The ladder diagram control system, can be monitored in 'real time'.
10. Modifications can take place whilst the PLC is on-line.
11. Simulation, that is 'off-line' modelling of the control system, using a computer to simulate the functions of the PLC. This facility is not available with Mitsubishi MEDOC.

1.3 PLC ladder diagram symbols

1. Inputs X

(a) Normally open contact

X1
—| |—

When an external source, for example an external switch, push button, relay contact, etc., operates then the corresponding ladder diagram contact or contacts, normally open, will close.

The X1 indicates that the external input is connected to input X1 of the PLC.

(b) Normally closed contact

—|/|—

When the external input connected to the PLC is operated, then the corresponding ladder diagram contact or contacts will open.

Note

Except for inputs concerned with safety (see page 101), an input device is normally wired such that, on being operated, it will supply a voltage to the input terminals of the PLC.

2. Outputs Y

Y0
—( )—

An external output device for example a power relay, a motor starter, an indicator, etc., can be connected to the output terminals of the PLC, in this case output Y0.

When the PLC operates output Y0, then the output device will be energized.

In the Mitsubishi FX range of PLCs, the Y output can be connected to the external device, using one of the following types:

(a) Relay output   FX-32MR
(b) Transistor output   FX-32MT
(c) Triac output   FX-32MS

3. Auxiliary Memory Coils M

M0
—( )—

An auxiliary memory coil can be used in PLC programs for a variety of reasons:

(a) To operate when the set of inputs which are connected to the M coil are correct.

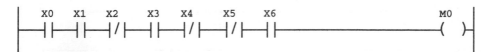

The Inputs corresponding to the normally open contacts, have been operated (i.e. X0, X1, X3, X6). The inputs corresponding to the normally closed contacts, have not been operated (i.e. X2, X4, X5). This information can then be used throughout the ladder diagram by simply using the contacts of the memory coil (i.e. M0) instead of having to repeat all of those contacts which caused the M coil to operate initially.

(b) As part of a latch circuit.

(c) As part of a shift register circuit.

1.4   Address ranges, Mitsubishi FX PLCs

The following range of addresses are those used for the FX-32M version 2 and above Mitsubishi PLCs

1. Inputs
   X0–X17 (octal) 16 inputs   expandable to 128 inputs
2. Outputs
   Y0–Y17 (octal) 16 outputs   expandable to 128 outputs
3. Timers
   T0–T199   0.1–3276.7 s
   T200–T245   0.01–327.67 s
   T246–T249   0.001–32.767 s retentive and battery backed
   T250–T255   0.01–3276.7 s retentive and battery backed
4. Counters
   C0–C99   general purpose
   C100–C199   battery backed
   C200–C219   bi-directional
   C220–C234   bi-directional and battery backed
   C235–C255   high speed
5. Auxiliary relays
   M0–M499   general purpose
   M500–M1535   battery backed
   M8000–M8255   special purpose (see page 128)
6. State Relays
   S0–S499   general purpose
   S500–S899   battery backed
   S900–S999   annunciator (see ANS instruction)
7. Data Registers
   D0–D199   general purpose
   D200–D999   battery backed
   D8000–D8255   diagnostic

1.5   Basic operation of a PLC system

To explain the basic operation of a PLC system, consider the following two lines of a ladder diagram program:

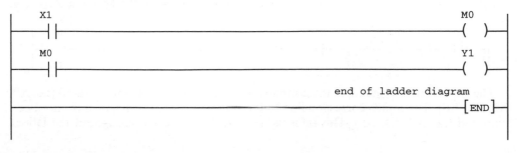

Principle of operation

1. When input X1 closes, this operates the internal memory coil M0.
2. On closing, the normally open contact of M0 will cause output Y1 to become energized.

Block diagram – PLC system

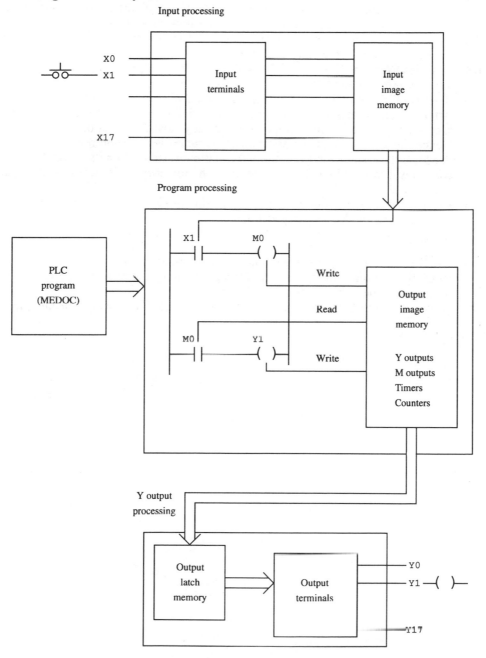

Principle of operation – PLC system

1. Input processing
   The PLC initially reads the ON/OFF condition of all of the Inputs used in the program. These conditions are then stored in the input image memory.
2. Program processing
   (a) The PLC then starts at the beginning of the PLC program and for each element of the program, it reads the actual logic state of that element, which is stored in either the input image memory or the output image memory.
   (b) If the required logic state is correct, that is X1 is ON, the PLC will move on to the next element in the rung, that is M0.
   (c) If X1 is ON, then a logic 1 will be written into the output image memory in the location reserved for M0.
   (d) If X1 is OFF, then a logic 0 is written into the M0 memory location.
   (e) After an output instruction has been processed, the first element on the next line is executed, which in this example is a normally closed contact of M0.
   (f) Hence the logic state of the M0 memory location is this time read, from and if this logic state is at logic 1 (i.e. the M0 coil is energized), then its normally closed contact will cause a logic 1 to be written to the memory location reserved for the output Y1.
   (g) However, if the logic contents are at logic 0 (i.e. M0 is not energized), then a logic 0 is written to the Y1 memory location

3. Output processing
   (a) Upon completion of the execution of all instructions, the contents of the Y memory locations within the output image memory are now transferred to the output latch memory and the output terminals.
   (b) Hence any output, which is designated to be ON (i.e. Y1) will become energized.

2
MEDOC software

Mitsubishi Electric (UK) Ltd have developed MS-DOS®-based software for use with their range of PLCs, known as MEDOC (Mitsubishi Electric Documentation). This software has all those facilities as described earlier, except for off-line simulation. It is menu based and in the opinion of many, including the author, very 'user friendly'.

2.1 Tree diagram – MEDOC operating system

The following diagram is a pictorial representation of the majority of MEDOC operating system commands.

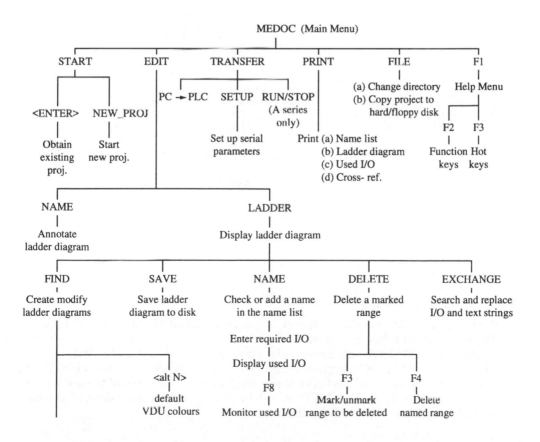

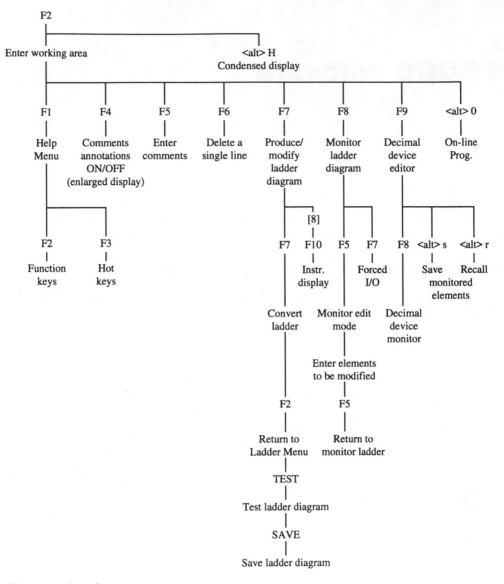

Figure continued

2.2 Initial start-up

1. It will be assumed that the computer has been switched ON and that the c:\root-directory prompt is being displayed.
2. Change to the MEDOC sub-directory by entering cd\ medoc <ENTER>.
3. To execute the MEDOC program, simply type in the following: medoc <ENTER>.
4. To indicate the pressing of the ENTER key, the following notation will be used <ent>.
5. After a few seconds, the logo MEDOC will be displayed for a short time, after which the following Main Menu will be displayed.

Main Menu

```
Select function
Start     Edit        Transfer      Print         Files      Options    Quit
Open      New_Proj    ListProj      PLC_chang     Save       Quick      Make_Lib
```

```
┌─────────────────────────────────────────────────────────┐
│              MELSEC  M E D O C                            │
│        Programming and Documentation System              │
│        for all Programmable Controllers from             │
│                                                          │
│        M i t s u b i s h i E l e c t r i c               │
│                                                          │
│                 Version 1.64b                            │
│        WORCESTER COLLEGE OF TECH No 2790                 │
│   Copyright (c) 1990, 1991, 1992, 1993, 1994, 1995       │
└─────────────────────────────────────────────────────────┘
```

```
Use cursor keys to select and then press ENTER or enter 1st letter
```

Help Menu

The Help Menu has been produced by Mitsubishi to help users find their way around the MEDOC software. It can be obtained at any time by pressing the function key <F1> and the information it will display will be relevant to what section of MEDOC is being used, prior to the pressing of <F1>.

The display below is obtained as follows:

1. Ensure the Main Menu is being displayed.
2. Ensure that Start is highlighted
3. Press <F1>.

```
Select function
┌─────┐
│Start│   Edit        Transfer      Print         Files      Options    Quit
└─────┘
Open      New_Proj    ListProj      PLC_chang     Save       Quick      Make_Lib
```

```
┌─────────────────── H E L P M E N U ───────────────────┐
│     Welcome as a user of the MELSEC MEDOC program package!│
│  MEDOC  is  a  program  for  the  development,  maintenance  and │
│  documentation  of  programs  for  MITSUBISHI  ELECTRIC  programmable │
│  controllers. The following PLC systems will be supported by this │
│  software version:                                       │
│                                                          │
│  F-12/F-20, F-40, F1/F2, F2U, FX0, FX, A0J2, A1, A1S, A2, A2C, A3, │
│            A3H, A3M A2A, A2A-S1, A3A                      │
│                                                          │
│  Before starting to use MEDOC, we recommend reading at least the │
│  introduction of the MEDOC manual. This provides an excellent │
│  overview                                                │
│  of the capabilities of MEDOC and highlights the basic differences │
│  between MEDOC and the usual programming units for MELSEC PLC- │
│  systems.                                                │
│                                                          │
│  PRESS [PgDn] TO READ NEXT PAGE!                         │
└───────── F1 = Help F2 = Function keys F3 = Hot keys ─────┘
        Use cursor keys to select and then press ENTER or
        enter 1st letter
```

2.3 Function keys

The function keys <F2> to <F9>, are used extensively for editing, modifying and monitoring a ladder diagram and hence it is necessary to be aware and remember the function of each of these keys.

To obtain a list of the function keys, carry out the following:

1. Press <F1> to obtain the Help Menu.
2. Press <F2>.

```
-------------------- FUNCTION-KEYS --------------------
F1  = Help
F2  = To/From Working Area
F3  = Mark start/stop
F4  = Range name & names in program editors
F5  = Insert a line
F6  = Delete Line
F7  = Ladder programming start/stop
F8  = Monitor
F9  = Keydefinitions - Instr/Ladder editor
F10 = Copy previous line (Name editor

           Hit Esc to exit this window
```

3. Press <esc> to return to the Main Menu.

2.4   Quick selection using the hot keys

From the tree diagram, it can be seen that MEDOC contains a large number of commands. To assist in speeding up the process of producing PLC projects, some of the more important commands can be immediately obtained from most places within MEDOC by pressing a single key. The keys which enable these more important functions to be immediately obtained, are known as hot keys.

The Hot Key Menu is obtained as follows:

1. Press <F1> to obtain the Help Menu.
2. Press <F3> to obtain the Hot Key Menu as shown below.

```
-------------- HOT-KEYS --------------
0 = Start Open
1 = Edit Instr
2 = Edit Ladder
3 = Edit Name
4 = Edit Param
5 = Transfer PLC
6 = Transfer GPP
7 = Print
8 = Files
9 = Quit Yes

Hit Esc to exit this window
```

3. Press <esc> twice to return to the Main Menu.

2.5   Quit

To exit from MEDOC at any time, carry out the following:

1. Press <esc> until the Main Menu as shown on page 9 is displayed.
2. Select Quit.
3. Select Yes.
4. The screen will now clear and just the c:\medoc or c:\medoc\trg prompt will be displayed.
5. Switch the computer OFF.
6. See also section 3.3 on creating a training sub-directory, c:\medoc\trg.

3
Using MEDOC to produce the PLC ladder diagram – FLASH1

3.1 PLC program – FLASH1

This program enables a PLC output (i.e. Y0) to be turned ON/OFF at a controlled rate. In this example the Y0 output will be ON for 1 second and then OFF for 1 second. It will be used to describe how a PLC ladder diagram can be produced, modified and tested. Then, using a Mitsubishi FX PLC, the program will be downloaded, run and monitored.

PLC ladder diagram

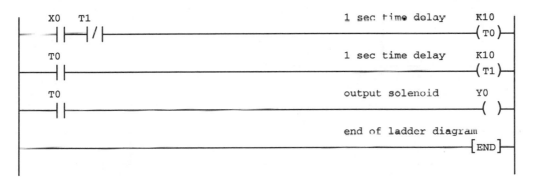

Principle of operation

1. On closing the input switch X0, the timer T0 coil will be energized via the normally closed contact of timer T1.
2. Timer T0 will now start timing out and after 1 second the timer will operate. This means:
   (a) Any T0 normally open contacts, -| |-, will close.
   (b) Any T0 normally closed contacts, -| / |-, will open.
3. There are two T0 contacts which are both normally open. Therefore both of them will close, causing the following to occur:
   (a) The timer T1 coil will become energized and start timing out.
   (b) Output Y0 will become energized, that is output Y0 will turn ON.
4. After timer T1 has been energized for 1 second, it will also operate and its normally closed contact will open, causing timer T0 to drop out.
5. With Timer T0 dropping out its normally open contact will now reopen causing:
   (a) Timer T1 to drop out.
   (b) Output Y0 to become de-energized, that is output Y0 will turn OFF.

6. Hence it can be seen that timer T1 is part of a 'cut-throat' circuit in that its operation immediately causes itself to drop out.
7. With timer T1 dropping out, its normally closed contact will reclose, causing the coil to become re-energized once again.
   Therefore as long as input X0 is closed, the operation will be constantly repeated.
8. Hence the output Y0 will flash ON/OFF every second.

FLASH1 waveforms

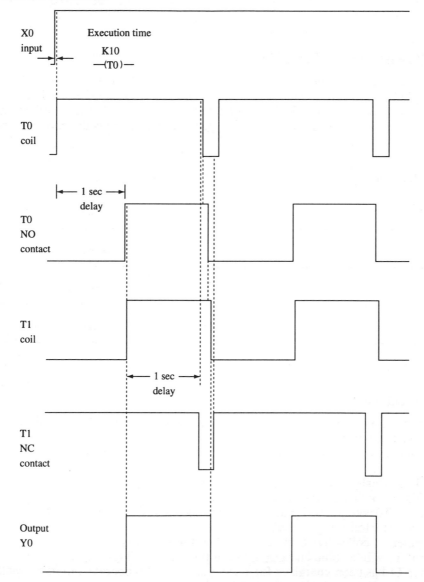

Note

The times taken to execute the instructions are very much magnified in comparison with the 1 second time delays of timers T0 and T1.

3.2 Selecting a function

1. It will be assumed that the initial start-up procedure has been carried out and the Main Menu is being displayed.

```
Select function
Start    Edit        Transfer     Print        Files    Options    Quit
Open     New_Proj    ListProj     PLC_chang    Save     Quick      Make_Lib
```

```
┌─────────────────────────────────────────────────────────┐
│               MELSEC M E D O C                            │
│                                                           │
│      Programming and Documentation System                │
│      for all Programmable Controllers from                │
│                                                           │
│      M i t s u b i s h i E l e c t r i c                  │
│              Version 1.64b                                │
│      WORCESTER COLLEGE OF TECH. No 2790                   │
│  Copyright (c) 1990, 1991, 1992, 1993, 1994, 1995         │
└─────────────────────────────────────────────────────────┘
```

```
       Use cursor keys to select and then press ENTER or enter 1st letter
```

2. The MEDOC software is based on a hierarchical menu selection process, in which the selection of one function leads to other related functions.
3. The selection process is carried out either by using the cursor keys, or by entering the first letter of the required function.
4. Determine where the following computer keyboard cursor keys are situated:
   - (a) Left cursor   ←
     horizontal cursor keys
   - (b) Right cursor   →
   - (c) Up cursor   ↑
     vertical cursor keys
   - (d) Down cursor   ↓
5. Using the horizontal cursor keys, select the required function followed by <ent>. Alternatively enter the initial letter of the function.
6. For example, to select the Files function.
   - (a) Press the horizontal right cursor → key until Files is highlighted. Then press <ent>.
   - (b) Alternatively press the lower case letter 'f'. However, this time, do not press <ent>.

3.3 Creating a training sub-directory

Where MEDOC is used within an organization, very often there are projects already stored on the computer's hard disk. Hence to ensure that those projects can in no way be accidentally altered or erased, it is advisable before starting a training programme to create a training sub-directory on the computer's hard disk. This is done as follows:
1. From the Main Menu select Files.

2. The display now becomes as shown below:

```
Select function                                                        Files
ListProj     Dir_Set     Copy      Erase      Rename     Save     Quick    Format
List current directory
```

```
                    ┌─────────────────────────────────────────────┐
                    │              MELSEC  M E D O C               │
                    │                                               │
                    │      Programming and Documentation System     │
                    │      for all Programmable Controllers from     │
                    │                                               │
                    │      M i t s u b i s h i E l e c t r i c      │
                    │                                               │
                    │              Version 1.64b                    │
                    │      WORCESTER COLLEGE OF TECH. No 2790        │
                    ├─────────────────────────────────────────────┤
                    │ Copyright (c) 1990, 1991, 1992, 1993, 1994, 1995 │
                    └─────────────────────────────────────────────┘
```

```
          Use cursor keys to select and then press ENTER or enter 1st letter
```

3. Select Dir_Set.
   The display now becomes:

```
Select function                                                        Files
ListProj     Dir_Set     Copy      Erase      Rename     Save     Quick    Format
Select source disk and directory
```

```
Enter new directory:     ┌──────────────────────────┐
                         │ C:\MEDOC\ _               │
                         └──────────────────────────┘
```

```
Directories under C:\MEDOC
LIST OF DIRECTORIES    <DIR>    DATE    TIME
```

4. Within the new directory window, enter at the flashing cursor: trg <ent>.
5. The display now becomes as shown below, with the following message displayed within the message window.

```
Select function                                                        Files
ListProj     Dir_Set     Copy      Erase      Rename     Save     Quick    Format
Select source disk and directory
```

```
Directory doesn't exist. Create directory (Y/N)? Y
```

```
Enter new directory:     ┌──────────────────────────┐
                         │ C:\MEDOC\TRG              │
                         └──────────────────────────┘
```

```
Directories under C:\MEDOC
LIST OF DIRECTORIES    <DIR>    DATE    TIME
```

6. Press <ent> to create the new training sub-directory.
7. The following message now appears:

```
    Do you wish to save directory setting (Y/N)? Y
```

8. Press <ent> so that the training sub-directory now becomes the default directory for saving and loading all further projects.
9. To return to a different sub-directory, repeat the above process, using the name of the required sub-directory.
10. Press <esc> to return to the Main Menu.

3.4 Opening a new project

To start, that is open, a new project, whose project name will be FLASH1, enter the following:
1. Select Start.
2. Select New_Proj.
3. A menu of all Mitsubishi PLC types now appears as shown below:

```
Select Function
Start
Open      New_proj     List     Proj     PLC_Chang     Save     Quick     Make Lib
Create new project
```

```
Select PLC-type and number of steps with the cursor keys, TAB and ENTER

        PLC-system          Steps                PLC-system          Steps

        F-12/20             320                  A0J2                3072
        F-40                890                  A1                  6143
        F1/F2               1000                 A1S(J)              6143
        F2U                 1000  2000           A1S-S1              6143
        FX0                 800                  A2(S)               6143
        FX                  2000                 A2C                 6143
        FX2C/Vup            2000                 A2S-S1              6143
        FX0N                2000                 A3                  6143
                                                 A2A(S)              6143
                                                 A2A(S)-S1           6143
                                                 A3A                 6143
```

4. The above PLC types covers the complete range of Mitsubishi PLCs to date.

Note

The limited F/FX version of the MEDOC software only enables projects to be produced for the F, FX and FX0 range of Mitsubishi PLCs. It does not cover the A series range of PLCs.
5. Using the vertical cursor keys select   FX   2000   <ent>.
6. A small window, within which a small cursor flashes on and off, is now displayed near the top of the screen, that is

```
Enter name of project:| _                    |
```

7. Within this window will be entered the project name. Enter flash1 <ent>.
8. The project name and type of PLC are now saved on disk and after a short delay, FLASH1 and FX will appear in white lettering at the top of the VDU screen.
9. Press <esc> to return to the Main Menu.

3.5 Ladder diagram – FLASH1

1. From the Main Menu, select Edit.
2. The Menu selection at the top of the screen now changes to the following:

```
Select function                          FLASH1           FX        Edit
Header              Name     Instr    Ladder    Param    Text    Other
Save        Copy
```

3. Select ladder.
4. The VDU display now changes to show the following blank ladder diagram. Ensure that the function Find has been selected, that is Find is highlighted.

```
Selectfunction or hit F2 to edit    FLASH1              FX         Ladder
  Find     Save     Name     Copy      Move     Delete   Exchange   Test
  Step     I/o      Text
```

		Steps used : 0	Steps left : 2000

```
|                                                                        |
|                                                                        |
|                                                                        |
|                                                                        |
|                                                                        |
|                                                                        |
|                                                                        |
|                                                                        |

  1        2        3        4        5        6        7        8        9

 ⊣⊢     ⊣/⊢     ⊔⊔     ⊔/⊔      |       —      —( )—   —[ ]—    P,I
```

5. The PLC symbols shown at the bottom of the screen are selected by entering the corresponding number above the symbol. For example:

   (a) Normally open contact   ⊣⊢   <1>
   (b) Normally closed contact   ⊣/⊢   <2>
   (c) Normally open parallel contact   ⊔⊔   <3>
   (d) Normally closed parallel contact ⊔/⊔   <4>
   (e) Vertical line | <5>
   (f) Horizontal Line   —   <6>
   (g) Solenoid/memory/timer coil   —( )—   <7>

6. Press <F2> to enter the ladder diagram's working area.
7. Press <F7> to select write mode.

The display on the VDU screen now becomes:

```
Working Area     Write     Offline   FLASH1                FX         Ladder
Find      Save   Name      Copy      Move      Delete      Exchange   Test
Step      I/o    Text
```

```
Write
Cursor
```

8. The ladder diagram FLASH1, as shown on page 11, will now be entered from the keyboard.
9. Enter 1, to select a normally open contact. At the bottom of the VDU screen, there now appears another window inside which is the symbol for a normally open contact.

```
X0
┤├
```

10. Enter the contact number X0.
11. The relay contact symbol and its associated contact number will be displayed on the screen, as shown above.
12. On pressing <ent>, the normally open contact X0, will appear on the ladder diagram, as shown below.

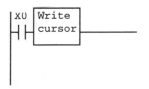

13. To enter the normally closed contact T1, enter the following:
    (a) 2
    (b) T1 <ent>
14. To enter timer T0, which will have a time delay of 1 second, carry out the following:
    (a) Enter 7, for a solenoid/memory/timer coil.
    (b) Enter T0 <ent> for timer T0.
    (c) Enter K10 <ent> for a 1 second delay.

```
K10
(T0)
```

15. The entering of a solenoid/memory/timer coil will cause the coil to be entered on the right hand side of the rung, thereby completing the rung.
16. PLC Diagram

17. Enter the following details for the second rung:
    (a) 1   ⊣⊢   T0 normally open contact
    (b) T0 <ent>
    (c) 7   ⊣ ⊢   solenoid/memory/timer coil
    (d) T1 <ent>   timer T1
    (e) K10   time delay = 1 second
18. PLC Diagram

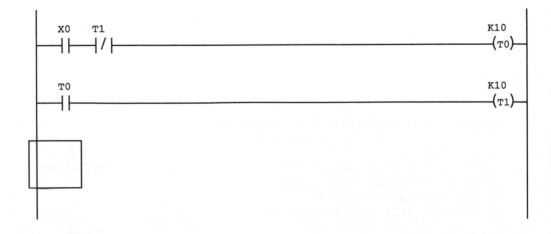

19. Enter the following details for the third rung:
   (a) 1   ⊣ ⊢   T0 normally open contact
   (b) T0 <ent>
   (c) <7>   ─(0)─   solenoid/memory/timer coil
   (d) Y0 <ent>   output solenoid Y0
20. PLC diagram

3.6 End of program

1. To end the ladder diagram, it is necessary to use the PLC instruction END.
2. To enter the END instruction, simply type in the following: end <ent>.
3. Complete ladder diagram

This completes the section, which describes how a PLC ladder diagram is produced.

3.7 Conversion to an instruction program

1. In the MEDOC memory, the PLC program is stored on disk as a set of instructions known as an instruction program or statement list. Hence, it is necessary to convert the ladder diagram into this type of program.
2. To carry out the conversion process, carry out the following: Enter <F7>

```
Working Area                        FLASH1          FX        Ladder
Find      Save     Name     Copy    Move    Delete  Exchange  Test
Step      I/o      Text
```

Conversion completed

3. The display now becomes as shown below:
4. Note the following:
   (a) The message Conversion completed.
   (b) At the start of each new rung is a step number.

3.8   Step numbers

All Mitsubishi PLCs have a certain memory capacity which is defined in steps. The maximum number of steps for the PLC determines the maximum size of the project, whether it is designed in ladder diagram form or as an instruction program.

As shown on page 16, the size of an FX project is 2000 steps and can be expanded to 4000 steps.

For simple input/output projects, for example FLASH1, the step requirements are as follows:

	Step value
Single input	1
Single output	1
Output contact	1
Internal memory – coil	1
Internal memory – contact	1
Timer coil and K value	3
Timer contact	1
Counter coil and K value	3
Counter contact	1
End	1

Note

Timers and counters in the FX series PLCs, require three steps:
1. The timer coil requires two steps.
2. The constant K value (i.e. the actual time delay is tenths of a second) requires one step.

Hence after the project FLASH1 has been converted, the step number at the start of each Line can be confirmed, by using the list above. The project FLASH1 uses a total of 12 steps (0–11 steps).

3.9   Saving a project

To save the project FLASH1 in the c:\medoc\trg sub-directory, carry out the following:

1. Press <esc>. The main heading in the top left corner will now change to the Select function:

```
Select function or hit F2 to edit   FLASH1              FX          Ladder
Find      Save     Name     Copy     Move      Delete    Exchange    Test
Step      I/o      Text
```

2. Select Save.
3. The program will now be saved to disk.
4. Below the ladder menu, the following message will now appear:

```
Program saved                              xxxxx bytes free on disk
```

where xxxxx is the number of available bytes left on the hard disk

3.10   Instruction programming

An instruction program is an alternative method for producing PLC programs. However, unless a programmer is very skilled at producing such programs it is very unlikely that a complex instruction program could be produced. Where MEDOC has been used to produce a PLC program using a ladder diagram, then the equivalent instruction program can be displayed.

Instruction program – FLASH1

To obtain the equivalent instruction program for FLASH1, which should still be the current project, carry out the following:

1. From the Main Menu select the following:
   (a) Edit.
   (b) Instruction.
2. Displayed on the screen will be the instruction program for FLASH1 as given below.

Ladder diagram – FLASH1

Instruction program – FLASH1

Step	Instr	I/O	Name
0	LD	X0	
1	ANI	T1	
2	OUT	T0	
		K10	
5	LD	T0	
6	OUT	T1	
		K10	
9	LD	T0	
10	OUT	Y0	
11	END		

Explanation – FLASH1 instruction program

1. Start of a rung
   (a) Where the first contact on each rung is a normally open contact, then the equivalent instruction will always be

   LD (Load).

   (b) Where the first contact on each rung is a normally closed contact, then the equivalent instruction will always be

   LDI (Load inverse).

2. Contacts in series
   Where there is more than one contact connected in series, then to obtain an output, all of the contacts must be correctly operated, that is

   X0 ON
   T1 OFF

   Hence for the timer coil T0 to be energized, input X0 is operated AND the input T1 is not operated. This is written in an instruction program as

   LD X0
   ANI T0

   Hence after the first contact on each rung, any additional series-connected contacts will be preceded by the following:

   AND   for all normally open contacts
   ANI   for all normally closed contacts

3. Outputs
   Each rung must be terminated by one or more outputs, that is:
   (a) Output solenoid   Y
   (b) Timer coil   T
   (c) Counter   C
   (d) Internal memory   M
   (e) Special instructions, that is

      Pulse   PLS
      Master contact   MC
      End of program   END

   (f) An advanced instruction   Refer to section 16.5

All outputs are preceded with the instruction OUT, followed by the output number and, if required, a constant K value. That is:

OUT   T0
       K10

This indicates that timer T0 has been programmed to give an ON time delay of 1 second.

3.11   Instruction search

Instruction search is an extremely useful facility, which is available within instruction programming, in that it enables a search to be carried out for a particular program instruction. This facility is not available with ladder diagram programming.

As will be shown in a later chapter an instruction IST is used in multi-sequence programming, and can only be used once in a program. Hence, where a ladder diagram contains a large number of steps and it is difficult to determine if a particular instruction such as IST is being used, then the instruction search facility can confirm whether or not it is in the program.

The following describes how, using the project FLASH1, a search is carried out for the instruction OUT.

1. It will be assumed that the program FLASH1 has been opened.

2. From the Main Menu select the following:
   (a) Edit.
   (b) Instruction.
3. Displayed on the screen will be the instruction program for FLASH1.

```
Select function or hit F2 to edit        FLASH1         FX              FIND
Step        I/o       Text
Search for a stepnumber
_____
Step        Instr     I/O        Name
0           LD        X0
1           ANI       T1
2           OUT       T0
                      K10
5           LD        T0
6           OUT       T1
                      K10
9           LD        T0
10          OUT       Y0
11          END
```

4. Select I/o and the message will change to:

```
Search for an I/O-number or I/O-name
```

5. Press <ent> and the following message is now displayed:

```
Start from beginning of program (Y/N)? Y
```

6. Press <ent> to confirm the search is to start from the beginning of the program.
7. The message now becomes

```
Search I/O name: _                Forward
```

8. Press <F10> to select the instruction search. The message now becomes:

```
Search Instruction: _             Forward
```

9. At the cursor position enter the instruction OUT <ent>.

10. The display now becomes as shown below and it can be seen that the cursor, ->, now appears alongside the first occurrence of the instruction OUT (i.e. at Step 2).

```
Select function or hit F2 to edit        FLASH1        FX         FIND
Step        I/o        Text
Search for a stepnumber
_____
    Step      Instr      I/O      Name
     0        LD         X0
     1        ANI        T1
 -> 2         OUT        T0
              K10
     5        LD         T0
     6        OUT        T1
              K10
     9        LD         T0
    10        OUT        Y0
    11        END
```

11. Repeatedly pressing <ent> will enable all occurrences of the instruction OUT to be found.

4
Modifications

Very often it is necessary to modify an existing ladder diagram. This may be caused by:

1. An incorrect entry on the ladder diagram.
2. Necessary improvements to the system as a whole.

To demonstrate the methods by which an existing ladder diagram can be modified, the diagram FLASH1 will be changed to the ladder diagram as shown below and its project name will be changed to FLASH2.

Modified ladder diagram – FLASH2

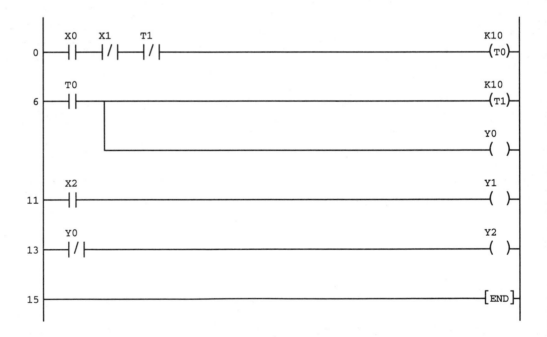

Modification details

As can be seen from the diagram for FLASH2, the modifications consist of the following:

1. An additional normally closed input X1 is inserted at rung 0.
2. A single contact of T0 feeds both timer T1 and output Y0.

3. An additional rung is inserted at rung 11. This consists of a normally open contact X2, connected to output coil Y1.
4. At rung 13, a normally closed contact of Y0 is used to energize output coil Y2. Hence as Y0 turns ON, then output Y2 turns OFF and vice versa.

4.1 Copying projects

This section describes how an existing project can be copied to a second project which has a different filename. This is required when modifying an existing project and yet still retaining a copy of the original ladder diagram. This is necessary in case the modifications do not work as expected and therefore the original project has to be reloaded into the PLC, so that production can be maintained.

Hence, prior to modifying the existing project FLASH1, it is necessary to copy FLASH1 into project FLASH2. This is done as follows:

1. From the Main Menu as shown on page 9, select Files.
2. Select Copy.
3. From the existing project list, select FLASH1.
4. The display now becomes as shown below.

Select function							Files
Listproj	Dir_Set	Copy	Erase	Rename	Save	Quick	Format
Copy projects							

Enter the name of the copy: | FLASH1 |

PROJECT	PC-type	Steps	Size	Name	Instr	Date	Time
FLASH1	FX	12	4572	TEST	OK	2-12-95	14:15

Note

(a) *FLASH1 is highlighted.*
(b) *Size refers to the total disk storage in bytes, which is being used for all of the files relating to the project FLASH1, that is*

FLASH1.NAM	4096 bytes
FLASH1.HDR	82 bytes
FLASH1.PRM	258 bytes
FLASH1.PRG	136 bytes
	4572 bytes

5. Enter the new project name: FLASH2 <ent>.

Select Function							Files
Listproj	Dir_Set	Copy	Erase	Rename	Save	Quick	Format
Copy projects							

Enter the name of the copy: | FLASH2 |

PROJECT	PC-type	Steps	Size	Name	Instr	Date	Time
FLASH1	FX	12	4572	TEST	OK	2-12-95	14:15

6. As the destination drive is not being changed press <ent>.
7. As the project is being stored in the c:\mcdoc\trg directory, press <ent> once more.
8. The following message is now displayed:

Project copied

This completes the section which describes how a project is copied to a new project having a different filename.

4.2 Listing saved projects

As a quick check to determine that the project FLASH2 has been saved, select Listproj from the Files menu.

```
Select function                                                          Files
Listproj        Dir_Set    Copy      Erase     Rename    Save    Quick    Format
Copy projects
```

A list of all the saved projects in the c:\medoc\trg directory will now appear:

```
Select Function                                                          Files
Listproj        Dir_Set    Copy      Erase     Rename    Save    Quick    Format
Copy projects
```
```
Project list
```

Project	PLC-type	Steps	Size	Name	Instr	Date	Time
FLASH1	FX	12	4572	TEST	TEST	2-12-95	14:15
FLASH2	FX	12	4572	TEST	TEST	2-12-95	16:50

4.3 Loading an existing project

Before carrying out any modifications to an existing project, it is necessary for the project to be loaded from the c:\medoc\trg directory into the memory of the computer.

To load the FLASH2 ladder diagram, carry out the following procedure:

1. Repeatedly press <esc> until the Main Menu is displayed, as shown on page 9.
2. Select Start.
3. Select Open.
4. Press <ent> to select an existing (old) project.
5. The display now becomes as shown below.

```
Select function
Start
Open        New_proj    List      Proj    PLC_Chang    Save    Quick    Make Lib
Create new project
```

```
Select a project with the cursor keys and ENTER. Turn page with PgUp and PgDn
```

PROJECT	PLC-type	Steps	Size	Name	Instr	Date	Time
FLASH1	FX	12	4572	TEST	TEST	2-12-95	14:15
FLASH2	FX	12	4572	TEST	TEST	2-12-95	16:50

6. Select FLASH2 <ent> from the displayed project list.
7. Press <esc> to return to the Main Menu.
8. Select Edit.
9. Select Ladder.
10. The ladder diagram for FLASH2 will now be displayed. This will be identical to FLASH1 since, as yet, no modifications have been carried out.

4.4 Modification of the ladder diagram FLASH2

Insertion of a new contact

1. Before any modifications can be carried out, it is necessary for the ladder diagram FLASH2 to be displayed on the screen.

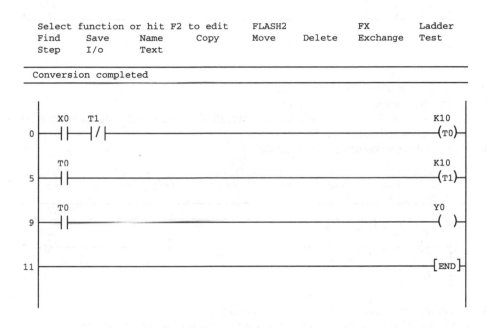

```
Select function or hit F2 to edit     FLASH2              FX          Ladder
Find      Save      Name      Copy      Move     Delete   Exchange    Test
Step      I/o       Text
```
Conversion completed

2. To insert the normally closed contact X1 between X0 and T1, it will be necessary to change from write mode to insert mode.
   Hence to insert contact X1, carry out the following:
   (a) Press <F2> to enter the working area.
   (b) Press <F7> to enter write mode.
   (c) Only the rung which is to be modified is now displayed. Also the small cursor is now replaced with the much larger write cursor.

   (d) Using the → key, position the write cursor over the normally closed contact T1.
3. Press the <ins> key.

4. In the top menu, the label Write is now replaced with Insert.

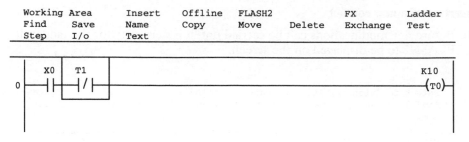

5. Press 2 for a normally closed contact.
6. Enter the contact name X1 <ent>.
7. Displayed on the screen will be the modified rung, which will now include the normally closed contact X1.
8. Press <ins> to return to write mode.

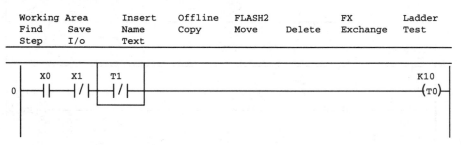

9. Press <F7> to enable the following to occur:
    (a) Convert the modified rung to its equivalent instruction program.
    (b) Note the Conversion completed message.
    (c) The display of the complete ladder diagram

Partly modified ladder diagram – I

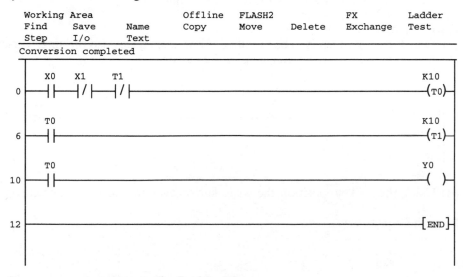

10. Press <esc> to return to the Ladder Menu.

4.5 Line numbers

In the descriptions which follow, references will be made to line numbers. A line number is the step number of the first element for that particular line. Therefore line numbers will not increase by one from one line to the next, but will depend on the number of steps used by the elements, for each line.

4.6 Addition of a new line to an existing line

To modify the ladder diagram to enable an additional line to be added to an existing rung (i.e. to enable the output Y0 to be parallel with the T1 output), carry out the following:

1. Ensure that the complete ladder diagram is displayed on the screen.
2. Press <F2> and, using the cursor keys, position the small cursor at the start of line 6.
3. Press <F7> and ensure the system is in write mode. If the label Insert is still present, then press <ins> to toggle back to write mode.
4. As before only a single rung will be displayed, as shown below.
5. Use the cursor key → to move the write cursor one position to the right.

6. Enter 5, to enable a vertical line to be drawn downwards.

7. Press the ↓ cursor key, to enable the write cursor to move down one line, as shown below.
8. Enter 7, to obtain an output coil.

9. Enter Y0 <ent>.
10. The additional rung will now be entered on the ladder diagram.
11. Press <F7> for the modification to be converted to an instruction program.
12. The ladder diagram FLASH2 now becomes

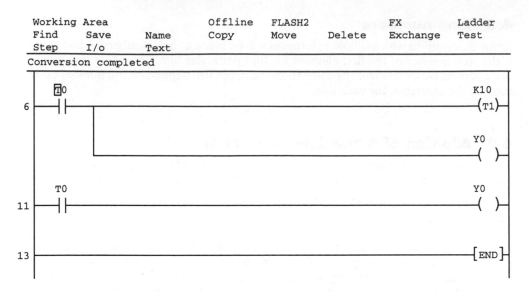

```
Working Area              Offline   FLASH2              FX        Ladder
Find     Save    Name     Copy      Move     Delete     Exchange  Test
Step     I/o     Text
```

Conversion completed

Note 1

The ladder diagram display starts at line 6, where the modification for the additional line was done.

To view the whole of the ladder diagram carry out the following:

(a) *Ensure that <F2> has been pressed and that, as shown above, the small working area cursor is being displayed.*

(b) *Press the ↑ cursor key, to display the complete ladder diagram starting at line 0.*

(c) *Alternatively, after pressing <F2>, enter 0 <ent>.*

Note 2

Entering <F2> followed by the required step number, will automatically find and move the display, to the start of the line containing the required step.

Partly modified ladder diagram – II

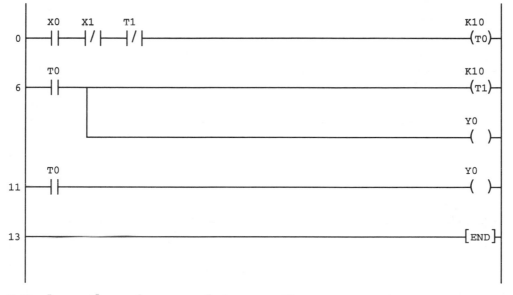

4.7   Insertion of a complete new line

The following notes describe how a complete rung can be inserted between line 6 and line 11 of the ladder diagram shown on page 32. This is done as follows:

1. Ensure the ladder diagram FLASH2 is displayed.
2. Press <F2> to enter the working area.
3. Using the cursor keys, position the small green cursor at the start of line 6.
4. Press <F7> to enter write mode.
5. Press the ↓ cursor key twice, to enable the write cursor to be underneath line 6, as shown below.

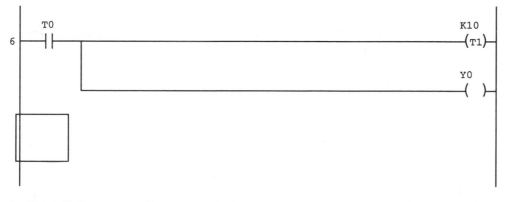

6. Enter 1, for a normally open contact.
7. Enter the contact number, X2 <ent>.
8. Enter 7, for a coil.
9. Enter the coil number, Y1 <ent>.
10. Press <F7> to convert to an instruction program.
11. Press <esc> to return to Select Function.

Partly modified ladder diagram – III

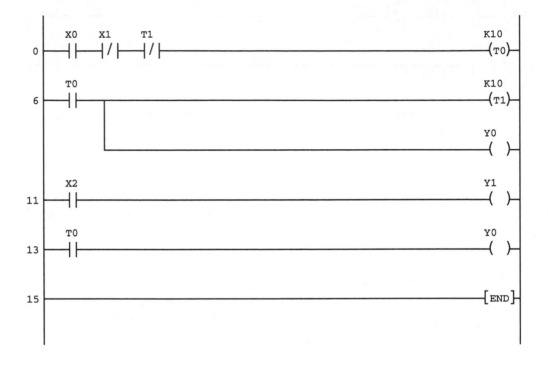

4.8 Change of contact type and I/O number

As can be seen from the modified FLASH2 diagram on page 26, the following modifications at line 13 are still to be done:

1. The normally open contact T0 is to be changed to a normally closed contact Y0.
2. The output coil Y0 is to be changed to Y2.

Change of contact type

The following notes describe how a normally open contact can be changed to a normally closed contact, and also be given a different contact number.

1. Press <F2> to enter the working area, use the cursor keys to position the small cursor at the start of line 13, and then carry out the following:
   (a) Press <F7> to enter write mode.
   (b) Enter 2, for a normally closed contact.
   (c) Enter Y0 <ent>, for the contact number.
2. The normally open contact T0 is now replaced with the normally closed contact Y0.
3. Press <F7> for the conversion of the modified contact.
4. The modified contact and contact number will now appear on the complete ladder diagram.

Partly modified ladder diagram – IV

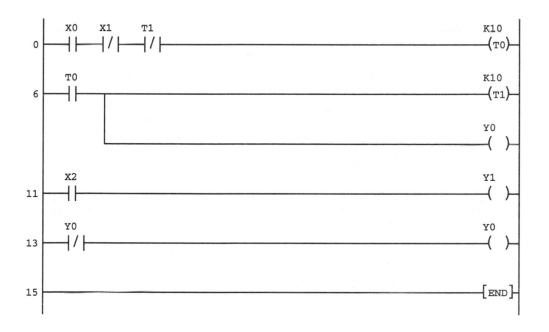

Change of I/O number

Changing the number of either an existing input contact or an output coil can be carried out simply without having to use the <F7> write mode. To demonstrate this, the contact number for the output coil on line 13, will be changed from Y0 to Y2 by carrying out the following:

1. Use the cursor keys to position the small cursor over the Y in Y0 at the end of line 13.
2. Press <ent>.
   A small grey window now appears above the output coil, within which is a flashing black cursor and the coil number Y0.

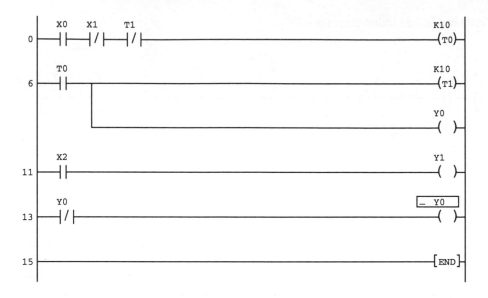

3. Enter Y2 <ent>.
4. The Y0 output coil number is now replaced with Y2.

Complete modified ladder diagram FLASH2

The modified ladder diagram FLASH2, should now be as shown below and also be identical to the ladder diagram as shown on page 26.

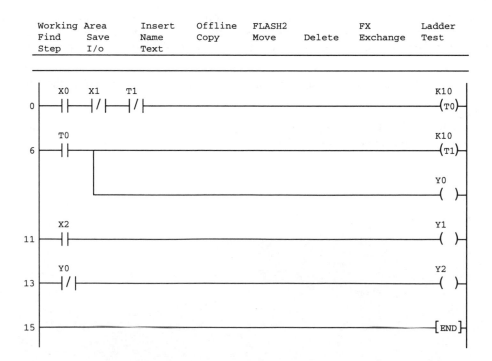

To save the modified ladder diagram FLASH2, carry out the following:

1. Press <esc> to return to Select Function.
2. Select Save <ent>.
3. The following message now appears in the window near the top of the screen;

Program saved	xxxxx bytes free on disk

4. The modified ladder diagram will now been saved onto the c: hard drive in the sub-directory c:\medoc\trg.

4.9 Deleting

When modifying a ladder diagram it is often necessary to delete one or more of the following:

1. An input contact.
2. Part of a rung.
3. A complete rung.
4. More than one rung simultaneously

The following describes how a copy of FLASH2 (i.e. FLASH3) is modified, to become as shown below.

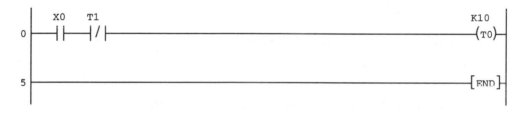

Copy FLASH2 to FLASH3

Before carying out any modifications, copy FLASH2 to FLASH3 using the procedure described on page 27.

4.10 Deleting an input contact

The following notes describe how a single input contact can be deleted using a horizontal line (6).

1. After copying FLASH2 to FLASH3, load the ladder diagram FLASH3, using the procedure described on page 28. This ensures that FLASH2 will not be modified, as it will be used later for testing a project.
2. From the Main Menu, open and then display the ladder diagram FLASH3.

Working	Area	Insert	Offline	FLASH3		FX	Ladder
Find	Save	Name	Copy	Move	Delete	Exchange	Test
Step	I/o	Text					

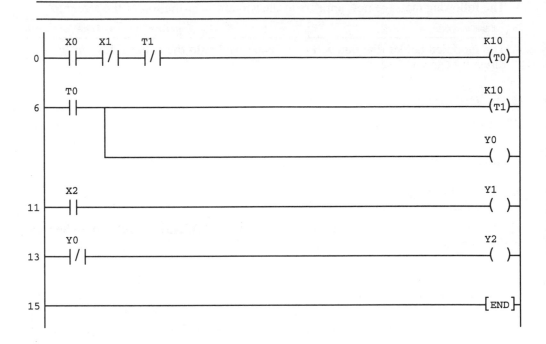

4.11   Procedure for deleting an input contact

To delete the normally closed contact X1 on rung 0 of FLASH3, carry out the following:

1. Ensure that the ladder diagram FLASH3 is being displayed.
2. Press <F2> to enter the working area.
3. Use the horizontal cursor keys to position the small cursor at the start of line 0.
4. Press <F7> to enter the Write mode. Ensure Write is being displayed and not Insert.
5. Use the → cursor key to position the write cursor over the normally closed contact X1.

6. Enter 6, to short-out the contact X1, that is ——.
7. Press <F7> for the modification to be converted to its equivalent instruction program.
8. The partly modified ladder diagram FLASH3 should be as shown at the top of page 39.

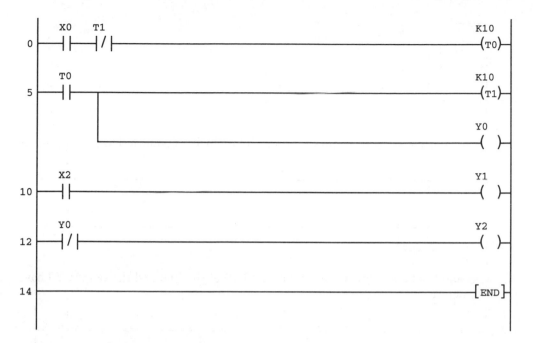

4.12 Deleting part of a line

Deleting just part of a rung can be done using the <space> bar.

1. The ladder diagram FLASH3 should appear as shown below, with the small cursor at the start of line 0.

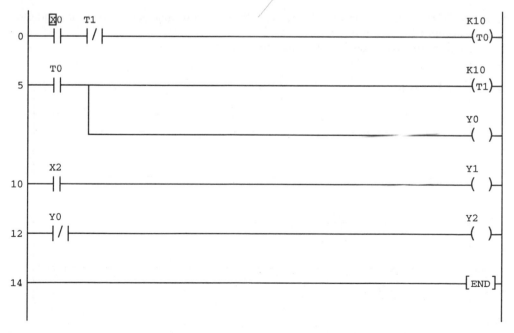

2. Move the cursor down to line 5 and press F7 to obtain the Write cursor.

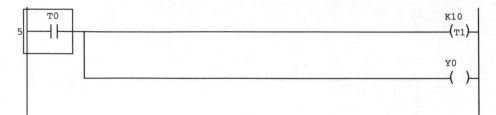

3. Position the Write cursor at the start of the line, which is connected to the output Y0.

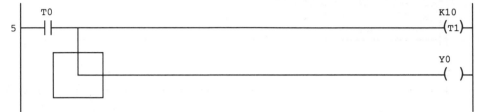

4. Press and hold down the <space> bar until all of the line and the output Y0 have been deleted.

5. Press F7 to convert the ladder diagram to its equivalent instruction program and also to renumber the line numbers.
6. The ladder diagram now becomes as shown below.

Note

One or more complete lines cannot be deleted, using the <space> bar.

4.13 Deleting a single line

If just a single line has to be deleted, this can be done using <F6>.

1. The ladder diagram FLASH3 should be as shown below, with the small cursor at the start of line 0.

2. Move the cursor down to line 9 and press <F6>.
3. All of line 9 is now highlighted in green.
4. Note the message

       Are you sure (Y/N)? Y

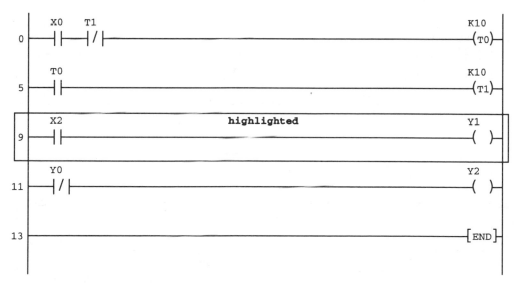

5. Since the default option is Yes, press <ent>.
6. The single line is now deleted and the step numbers are renumbered.

4.14 Deleting multiple lines

To delete more than one line, requires the use of the delete option. The following notes describe how to delete Lines 5–9 simultaneously.

1. The ladder diagram FLASH3 should be as shown below.

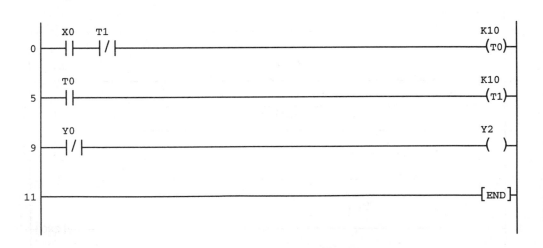

2. Select Delete to obtain the following:

```
Select function or hit F2 to edit      FLASH3          FX         Ladder
Find     Save     Name     Copy      Move      Delete    Exchange   Test
Step     I/o      Text
Delete a marked range or a range with a name in this project
F3 : Mark/Unmark  Enter : Perform command      F4 : Range marking
```

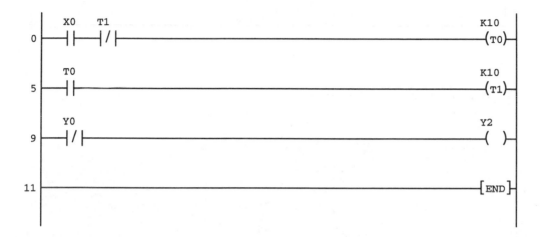

3. Note the message

   `F3: Mark/Unmark Enter: Perform command F4: Range marking`

4. Press <F2> to obtain the small cursor and move the cursor down to line 5.
5. Press <F3> and all of line 5 now becomes highlighted.
6. Press the down cursor ↓ once more and press <F3>.
7. Both lines 5 and 9 now become highlighted.

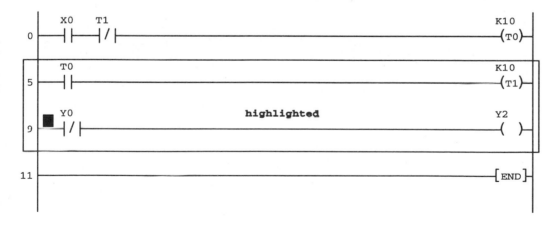

8. Press <ent>.
9. The following message is now displayed:

   `Are you sure (Y/N)? Y`

10. Press <ent> and both lines will be deleted.

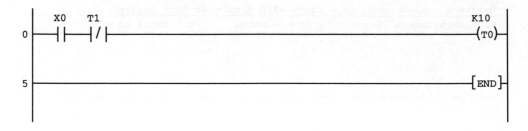

11. Save what remains of FLASH3.

5
Program testing

To check for errors, MEDOC provides a TEST facility which enables the following tests to be carried out:

1. Validity of I/O numbers.
2. Validity of the instructions for the type of PLC being specified.
3. Missing parameters for timers, counters and data instructions.
4. Correct use of jump instructions.
5. Correct use of master control (MC) and master control reset (MCR).
6. Inclusion of the END instruction.

If an error is detected, the test is terminated and the error is highlighted on the ladder diagram.

When a PLC ladder diagram is being developed and the diagram is being entered from the keyboard, then should an incorrect I/O, timer or counter number be entered, an error message will be immediately displayed. However, if the PLC is changed to a different type (see page 47) and if it uses a different range of numbers, then an error will occur when the program is tested.

5.1 Testing a project containing no errors

1. Open and display the ladder diagram FLASH2.

```
Select function or hit F2 to edit    FLASH2          FX          Ladder
Find      Save       Name      Copy      Move      Delete    Exchange    Test
Step      I/o        Text
```

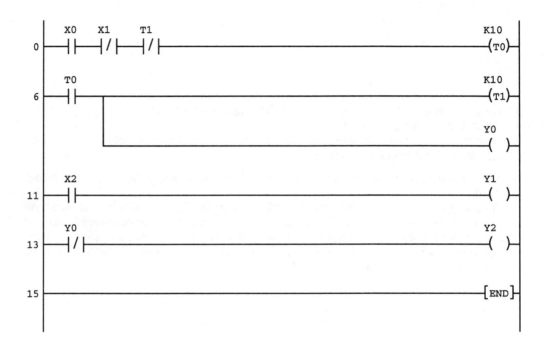

2. From the ladder menu select Test.
3. The display now becomes as shown on the facing page.

```
Select function or hit F2 to edit    FLASH2           FX        Ladder
Find     Save      Name      Copy       Move    Delete  Exchange  Test
Step     I/o       Text
Start from beginning of program (Y/N) ? Y
```

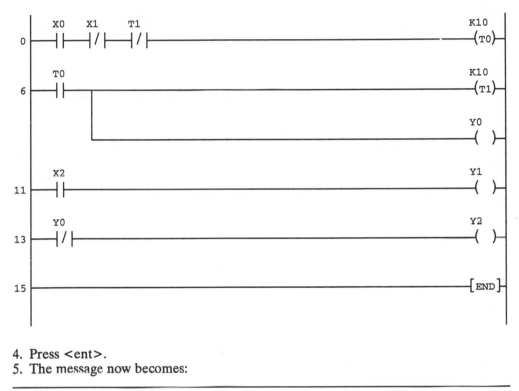

4. Press <ent>.
5. The message now becomes:

```
No errors found
```

6. The test confirms, that there are no errors in FLASH2.

5.2 Change of PLC type

The following describes how a project initially designed for an FX PLC displays errors when tested for use with an F1/F2 PLC.

1. Copy the project FLASH2 to TEST1. (The procedure for copying files is described on page 27.)
2. After the file has been copied, press <esc> until the Main Menu is displayed.
3. Select Start.
4. Press <ent> once more to obtain the project list
5. Select TEST1 <ent>.
6. Select PLC_Chang. (i.e. change of PLC).
7. From the PLC menu select F1/F2 <ent>. Enter Y to confirm the change.
8. Press <esc> and then display the ladder diagram TEST1.
9. Select Test from the Ladder Menu.
10. The ladder diagram TEST1 now becomes as shown overleaf.

Ladder diagram – TEST1

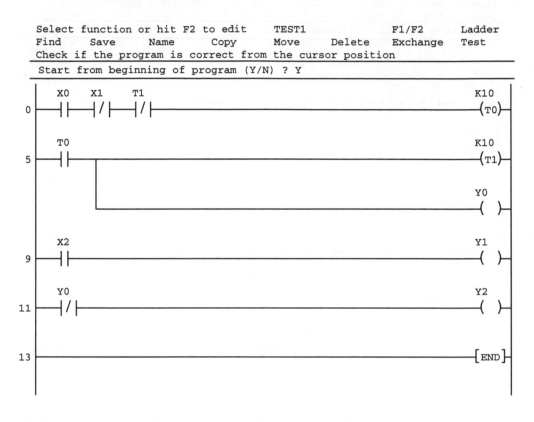

```
Select function or hit F2 to edit     TEST1              F1/F2      Ladder
Find     Save     Name     Copy       Move     Delete    Exchange   Test
Check if the program is correct from the cursor position
Start from beginning of program (Y/N) ? Y
```

11. Press <ent> to test the project from the beginning of the program.
12. The following message is now displayed:

```
Invalid I/O number
```

13. Also on line 0, a small cursor will appear around the normally closed contact T1.
    This indicates where the first error has been detected.
    For the F1/F2 range of PLCs, the timers are numbered from T50.
14. It would now be necessary to change all of the FX numbers to those for an F1/F2
    PLC, before the test facility would indicate no errors.

5.3 Exchanging I/O numbers

Where a project has been changed to a different PLC (i.e. from an FX to an F1/F2) then since the two PLCs use different numbering schemes, it is necessary for the element numbers to be changed.

Instead of changing each number on the ladder diagram one by one, which is a time-consuming process, the changes can be done more quickly using the Exchange function.

1. Ensure the ladder diagram TEST1, which uses an F1/F2 PLC, is displayed.
2. From the Ladder Menu select Exchange. The display now becomes as shown below.

```
Select function or hit F2 to edit    TEST1           F1/F2      Exchange
I/o      Text
Exchange an I/O - number from cursor position and to the end of program
```

3. Select I/o.
4. The following message is now displayed.

```
Start from the beginning of the program (Y/N)? Y
```

5. Press <ent> to start the exchange from the beginning of the program.
6. The message now changes to:

```
Change from: _
```

7. Enter t0 <ent>. This is the first timer number which is to be changed.

```
Batch Change (Y/N)? N
```

8. Press Y to confirm that all of the timer numbers are to be changed.

```
Batch end: _
```

9. Enter t1 <ent>. This is the last timer number which is to be changed.

```
to: _
```

10. Enter t50 <ent>. This is first timer number which is to be used by the F1/F2 series PLC.
11. The message now becomes:

```
Change one by one (Y/N)? Y
```

12. Press <ent> to enable the timer numbers to be changed one at a time.
13. Note that the normally closed timer contact T1, on line 0, is now highlighted.
14. Press <ent> to confirm the change. The normally closed contact T1 now changes to T51.
15. Continue pressing <ent> until all of the timer numbers have been changed to those numbers which are required for use with an F1/F2 series PLC.
16. When all of the Timer numbers have been changed, the following Message is displayed:

```
String T0 not found
```

17. Press <esc>.
18. Select Find.
19. Press <F2> and move the cursor to the start of the ladder diagram so that all of the ladder diagram can be displayed.
20. Press <esc> and the ladder diagram will be as shown below.

5.4 Exchange of output number

Repeat the test procedure on the modified ladder diagram TEST1. Note that there are still errors, however, as the Y output numbers on the F1/F2 series PLCs start from Y430.

Use the Exchange procedure to change the Y output numbers to those shown on the ladder diagram below (i.e. change Y0–Y2 to Y430–Y432).

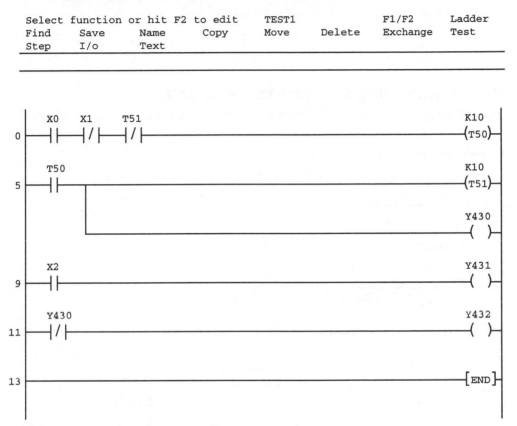

```
Select function or hit F2 to edit    TEST1                F1/F2     Ladder
Find      Save      Name      Copy    Move      Delete     Exchange  Test
Step      I/o       Text
```

6
Serial transfer of programs

6.1 Downloading a project to a PLC unit

The following notes describe how the project FLASH1 is downloaded to an FX PLC.

Circuit diagram

Connect the computer to the FX PLC as shown in the diagram below.

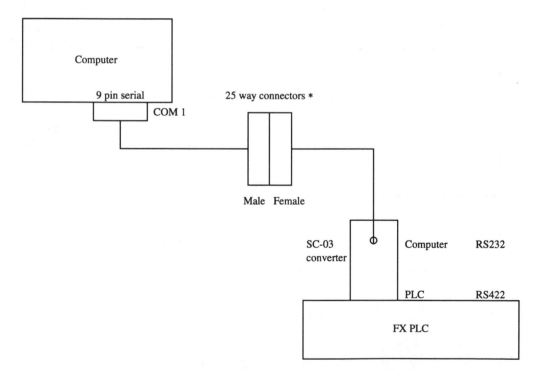

Note

Some of the later versions of the SC-03, are supplied with nine-way connectors.

1. Connect up the computer to the FX PLC, as shown in the circuit diagram.
2. Ensure the PLC is switched ON and that it is NOT in thc run mode.
3. Load the project FLASH1 and display the ladder diagram.
4. Carry out the test procedure and if there are no errors select Save.

5. Press <esc> until the Main Menu is displayed.
6. Select Transfer.
7. The display now becomes

```
Select function or hit F2 to edit      FLASH1          FX       Transfer
PLC         GPP          Other    Run/Stop   Setup   Eprom   A7BDE
Medoc>PL    PLC>Medoc    Verify   Run/Stop
```

```
PLC Transfer Menu
→  Program
   Comment
```

8. Select PLC <ent>.
9. Ensure that Medoc>PLC has been selected.
10. Press <ent>.
11. Press <Y>, if you are sure the transfer is to proceed.
12. Press <Y> to verify. This is to check that the program stored in the FX PLC will be identical to the computer program.
13. As the program is being downloaded to the FX PLC, the number of steps transferred will be displayed in the message window as an incrementing count from 0 to 2000 steps.
14. After the project has been successfully downloaded to the FX PLC the following messages will be displayed:

    (a) `Comparing Parameters No errors found Hit any key to proceed`

    Press <space bar>.

    (b) `Comparing Main Program No errors found Hit any key to proceed`

    Press <space bar>.

15. If there are any difficulties in downloading the program, retry without verifying the program.
16. If the program is successfully downloaded without verification, then the following message is displayed:

    `Transfer Completed`

Difficulties when downloading

Should there be any difficulties when a program is being downloaded then this could be caused by the following:

1. Hardware.
2. Software.

Hardware

If there is a hardware problem with the serial link, then the following message will be displayed:

`No reply from PLC system.`

If this message is obtained, then carefully check the SC-03 connection from the computer's COM1 serial output to the 25 way input connector of the PLC.

Software

If there appears to be a problem with the software, then check that the serial transmission parameters are correct.

From the Transfer Menu select Setup. The VDU display now becomes as shown below.

```
Select function or hit F2 to edit      FLASH1              FX           Transfer
PLC     GPP     Other     Run/Stop      Setup      Eprom    A7BDE
Communication setup for all PLC:s and AJ71
```

```
          Communication Setup
    ⇒  PLC - system            FX
       Bit rate                9600
       Word length             7
       Parity                  Even
       Stopbits                1
       Station                 0

       Port                    COM1

       Set default settings
```

Serial communications port COM2

On many computer installations the serial port COM1 is used for the serial mouse. If it is not convenient to remove the mouse and the computer has a second serial communications port (i.e. COM2) then this can be used for transferring programs from the computer to the PLC.

To do this, it is necessary to change the communication setup parameter from COM1 to COM2:

1. Ensure the setup parameters are being displayed.
2. Move the cursor down to Port.
3. Press the <space> bar to change to COM2.
4. Press <esc> to return to the Transfer Menu.
5. The display now becomes as shown below.

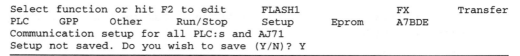

```
Select function or hit F2 to edit      FLASH1              FX           Transfer
PLC     GPP     Other     Run/Stop      Setup      Eprom    A7BDE
Communication setup for all PLC:s and AJ71
Setup not saved. Do you wish to save (Y/N)? Y
```

```
          Communication Setup
    ⇒  PLC - system            FX
       Bit rate                9600
       Word length             7
       Parity                  Even
       Stopbits                1
       Station                 0
       Port                    COM2
       Set default settings
```

6. Press <ent> to confirm the change to the setup parameters.

6.2 Verification

Situations may arise when, owing to extensive modifications to a PLC project, the program in the PLC may be different from that stored on disk. This is really a failure in good housekeeping practice (see Chapter 13). However, it is possible to verify that the programs stored in the PLC and on disk are identical, and if they are not identical, what the differences are.

To demonstrate the verify facility, which is in Transfer, the projects FLASH1 and FLASH2 will be used:

1. Currently, the project FLASH1 has been downloaded to the PLC.
2. Return to the Main Menu and open the project FLASH2.
3. Press <esc> and select Transfer.
4. Select PLC.
5. The display now becomes as shown below.

```
Select function or hit F2 to edit              FLASH2     FX       PLC
Medoc>PLC       PLC>Medoc     Verify       Run/Stop
Write a program into PLC from MEDOC memory
```

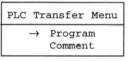

6. Select Verify and the program in the PLC will immediately be compared with the program in MEDOC memory.
7. Note the message:

```
Comparing Parameters No errors found Hit any key to continue
```

8. Press the <space> bar and the display now becomes
```
Select function or hit F2 to edit              FLASH2     FX       PLC
Medoc>PLC       PLC>Medoc     Verify       Run/Stop
Compare program in PLC with MEDOC program and display errors

Comparing Main Program Error Found Hit any key to continue

Difference at step: 1
Difference at step: 2
Difference at step: 3
Difference at step: 4
Difference at step: 5
Difference at step: 6
Difference at step: 7
Difference at step: 8
Difference at step: 9
Difference at step: 11
Difference at step: 12
Difference at step: 13
Difference at step: 14
Difference at step: 15
```

9. As expected, the two projects FLASH1 and FLASH2 are quite different.

If this situation had occurred with an industrial-based PLC project, it would obviously cause some concern as to why the PLC program and the program saved on disk were so different.

6.3 Uploading a program

Circumstances can arise when it is necessary to know what program is stored in the PLC itself. This may be due to a number of modifications being made to the original program but those changes have not been fully documented and saved on the master disks. Hence, after verifying that the project in the PLC is different from that stored on disk, then the working program within the PLC must be uploaded to MEDOC and stored on the master disks.

The following describes how the project FLASH1 is uploaded from the FX PLC and saved as FLASH4.

1. From the Main Menu, select Start and then open a new project. This is described on page 16.
2. Select the type of PLC being used and then enter a suitable filename. Enter flash4
3. The display will now become as shown below.

```
Select function                       FLASH4            FX              Start
Open      New_Proj    PLC_Chang    Save      Quick    Make_Lib
Create new project
```
```
New project created
```

```
Enter name of project: FLASH4
```

PLC-system	Steps		PLC-system	Steps
F-12/20	320		AOJ2	3072
F-40	890		A1	6143
F1/F2	1000		A1S(J)	6143
F2U	1000	2000	A1S-S1	6143
FX0	800		A2(S)	6143
FX	2000		A2C	6143
FX2C/Vup	2000		A2S-S1	6143
FX0N	2000		A3	6143
			A2A(S)	6143
			A2A(S)-S1	6143
			A3A	6143

4. Connect the computer to the FX PLC as shown in the diagram on page 52.
5. Press <esc> and, from the Main Menu, select Transfer.
6. Select PLC followed by PLC>Medoc.
7. The display then becomes as shown below.

```
Select function or hit F2 to edit       FLASH4        FX        PLC

Medoc>PLC  | PLC>Medoc |  Verify
```
```
Read a program from PLC into MEDOC memory
```
```
Are you sure (Y/N)? Y
```

```
          PLC Transfer Menu
           →   Program
               Comment
```

8. Press <ent> to confirm the program is to be transferred from the PLC to the computer.
9. Note the transfer step numbers will go from 0 to 2000 as the program is uploaded.
10. Press <esc> twice to return to the Main Menu.
11. Select Edit, then Ladder and note that FLASH4 is identical to FLASH1.

7
Monitoring a ladder diagram

After a project has been downloaded to the FX PLC or uploaded from the PLC, it is possible to monitor the ladder diagram in 'real time'.

To monitor the project FLASH1, carry out the following:

1. Open and display the ladder diagram FLASH1.
2. Connect an input switch box similar to the one shown below, to the PLC.

Input switch box – wiring diagram

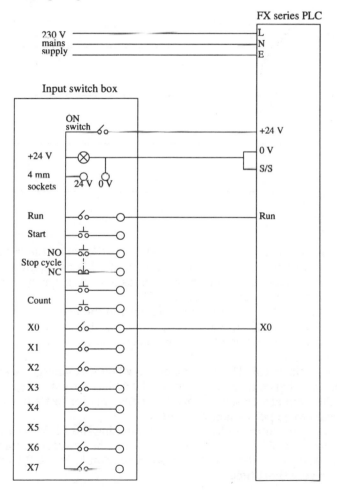

3. Press <F2> to enter the Working Area.
4. Press <F8> for monitor.
5. On the display the message Monitor will be flashing ON and OFF.
6. Connect a lead from the X0 4 mm socket on the switch box to the X0 input on the PLC. Operate the X0 switch.
7. The ladder diagram display will now monitor the inputs and outputs of FLASH1. This is done by indicating with a green square those inputs or internal contacts, which are closed, and with a green rectangle those solenoid/timer outputs, which are energized.
8. At the bottom of the display are the incrementing times, which indicate in tenths of a second how much time has elapsed since each timer coil was energized.
   Once a timer's countup constant has been reached, that is its specified delay has elapsed, then that timer's contacts will operate.
   (a) A normally open contact: will close.
   (b) A normally closed contact: will open.
9. If the ladder diagram is displayed over more than one screen, it is possible to monitor the required part of the diagram by using the Page Up and Page Down keys.

Monitor details

1. The monitor display appears to show that at line 0, the coil of timer T0 is permanently energized and that the normally closed contact of T1 is not opening.
2. This is due to the fact that when timer T1 times out, its normally closed contact does open and breaks the circuit to timer coil T0.
3. This causes timer T0 to drop out immediately and the two T0 contacts will open.
4. At line 5, the opening of the T0 contact, will break the circuit to timer coil T1.
5. The normally closed contact of T1 now remakes and, in doing so, will cause the T0 coil to re-energize.
6. The time from timer coil T0 dropping out to when it re-energizes will be only a few milliseconds and hence it appears that the T0 coil is permanently energized.
7. Similarly, the normally closed contact T1 opens only for just a few milliseconds and hence appears to be permanently closed.
8. This effect can be confirmed by carefully examining the FLASH1 waveforms, which are shown opposite. Although not drawn to scale, the waveforms confirm that the T0 coil is only de-energized for a very short time. Similarly the T1 contacts are only opened for a very short time.

FLASH1 waveforms

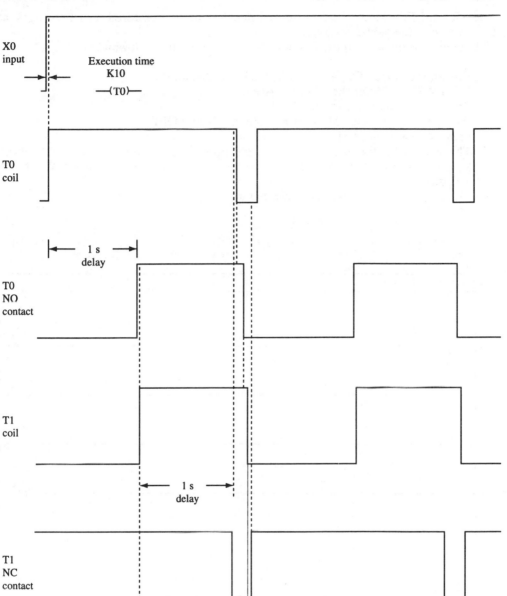

7.1 Monitor edit mode

The Monitor Edit Mode, enables up to 16 devices to be monitored over two pages, at the bottom of the ladder diagram.

To enter this mode from the Ladder Menu, carry out the following:

1. Ensure the ladder diagram FLASH1 is being displayed.
2. Press <F2> to enter the Working Area.
3. Press <F8> to enter Monitor Mode.
4. Wait until the message Monitor is flashing ON and OFF.
5. Press <F5> to enter Monitor Edit Mode.
   This will enable the names of up to eight program elements to be entered, whose logic states or contents are required to be monitored whilst the program is being executed.
6. The display now becomes as shown below.

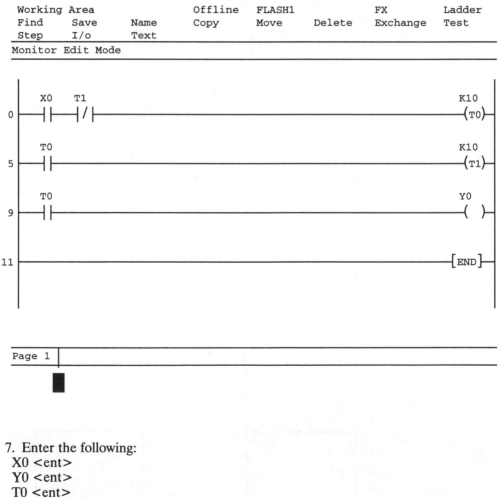

7. Enter the following:
   X0 <ent>
   Y0 <ent>
   T0 <ent>
   T1 <ent>

8. Press <F5> to return to Monitor Mode.
9. The display now becomes as shown below.

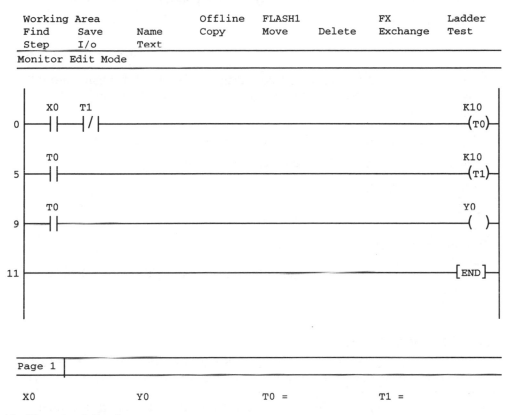

```
Working Area                Offline   FLASH1              FX          Ladder
Find      Save     Name     Copy      Move      Delete    Exchange    Test
Step      I/o      Text
Monitor Edit Mode
```

10. Note the following:
    (a) Whenever the input X0 operates, this is shown by a green square around X0.
    (b) Whenever the output Y0 operates, this is shown also by a green square around Y0.
    (c) The incrementing values of timers T0 and T1.
    (d) Monitor page 1.

7.2 Monitor pages

As mentioned previously, a total of 16 elements can be entered and monitored.

In monitor edit mode it is possible to access two monitor pages (i.e. page 1 and page 2). Each page, which can monitor up to eight elements, is separately displayed at the bottom of the Ladder Diagram. To switch between the two monitor pages, use the up ↑ and down ↓ cursor keys.

1. From Monitor Mode, press the down cursor key and note that the monitor page now changes to page 2.
2. Press <F5> to enter Monitor Edit Mode.
3. Enter the following elements:
    (a) X0
    (b) Y0
4. Press <F8> and note that, this time, only X0 and Y0 are being monitored.
5. To monitor the elements on page 1, press the up ↑ cursor key.

7.3 Deleting monitored elements

To delete a single monitored element, carry out the following:

1. From Ladder Mode enter:
   (a) F2
   (b) F8
   (c) F5
   The first two are not needed if the ladder diagram is currently being monitored.
2. Using the cursor keys position the cursor just after the element which is to be deleted. Do not press <ent>.
3. Press <F6>.
4. The selected element will now be deleted from the bottom of the screen.

To delete all of the monitored elements, carry out the following:

1. From Ladder Mode enter:
   (a) F2
   (b) F8
   (c) F5
   The first two are not needed if the ladder diagram is currently being monitored.
2. Enter <shift F6>.
3. All of the elements which were monitoring the program, will now be deleted from the bottom of the screen.
4. Press <F5> to return to Monitor Mode.

7.4 Decimal device monitor

The Decimal Device Monitor enables selected device elements to be monitored without the use of a ladder diagram. The advantage of this type of monitor is that more than eight elements can be monitored simultaneously.

To use the Decimal Device Editor, carry out the following from Ladder Mode:

1. Enter the following:
   (a) F2
   (b) F9
   (c) <shift F6>. This clears any elements which were previously entered.
2. The display now becomes as shown below.

Working	Area		Offline	FLASH1		FX	Ladder
Find	Save	Name	Copy	Move	Delete	Exchange	Test
Step	I/o	Text					

```
                             ──────── Device Monitor ────────

     I/O      Name    Decimal    Pre/ASC    Hex     FEDC   BA98   7654   3210

 ⇒
```

3. Enter the following elements:
   X0 <ent>
   T0 <ent>
   T1 <ent>
4. The display now becomes as shown below.
5. If additional elements are to be inserted within the list, then carry out the following.

Working	Area		Offline	FLASH1		FX	Ladder
Find	Save	Name	Copy	Move	Delete	Exchange	Test
Step	I/o	Text					

_____ Device Monitor _____

I/O	Name	Decimal	Pre/ASC	Hex	FEDC	BA98	7654	3210
X0								
T0								
T1								

⇒

Move the cursor to where the additional element is to be inserted and press <F5>
<ent>. This causes a rectangular window to be displayed at the cursor position.

Working	Area		Offline	FLASH1		FX	Ladder
Find	Save	Name	Copy	Move	Delete	Exchange	Test
Step	I/o	Text					

_____ Device Monitor _____

I/O	Name	Decimal	Pre/ASC	Hex	FEDC	BA98	7654	3210
X0								

⇒ [_   ]

T0								
T1								

6. Enter the required element within this window, that is Y0 <ent>.

Working Area			Offline	FLASH1		FX	Ladder
Find	Save	Name	Copy	Move	Delete	Exchange	Test
Step	I/o	Text					

```
───────────────────── Device Monitor ─────────────────────
    I/O      Name     Decimal     Pre/ASC     Hex      FEDC     BA98   7654   3210
    X0

    Y0

⇒   T0

    T1



```

Monitoring in decimal device mode

1. To monitor the devices using Decimal Monitoring, press the following:
   (a) <F2> (already entered, see above)
   (b) <F9> (already entered, see above)
   (c) <F8>
2. The display now becomes as shown below.

Working Area			Offline	FLASH1		FX	Ladder
Find	Save	Name	Copy	Move	Delete	Exchange	Test
Step	I/o	Text					

| Monitor | | | | | | Decimal | | |

```
───────────────────── Device Monitor ─────────────────────
```

I/O	Name	Decimal	Pre/ASC	Hex	FEDC	BA98	7654	3210	
X0		1	☺	1				1	
Y0		1	☺	1				1	*
T0		10	K10	A	0000	0000	0000	1010	*
T1		2	K1	2	0000	0000	0000	0010	*

*Indicates these values are changing, whilst being monitored
3. Note the following:
   (a) When the input X0 operates, a green square appears around X0.
   (b) When the output Y0 operates, a green square appears around Y0.
   (c) At the end of the time delay for T0, a green square appears around T0.
   (d) The incrementing values of timers T0 and T1.

7.5 Saving monitored elements

Where a large project is causing problems and finding the fault is taking a long time, it is advisable to save the list of elements which are being monitored. This ensures that later, when another attempt is made to determine what the problems are, the list of monitored elements does not have to be re-cntered.

To save the the list of monitored elements, carry out the following:

1. Ensure that the display is of FLASH1 in Device Mode, but not in Monitor Mode.
2. If in Monitor Mode, then quit by pressing <esc>.
3. The display, except for the monitored values, should be as shown below.

```
Working Area                  Offline    FLASH1                FX         Ladder
Find      Save    Name        Copy       Move      Delete      Exchange   Test
Step      I/o     Text
─────────────────────────────────────────────────────────────────────────────
                      ──────────── Device Monitor ────────────
   ┌───────────────────────────────────────────────────────────────────┐
   │  I/O     Name    Decimal    Pre/ASC     Hex    FEDC   BA98 7654 3210│
   │  X0               1           ☺          1                        1 │
   │  Y0               1           ☺          1                        1 │
   │  T0              10          K10         A     0000   0000 0000 1010│
   │  T1               2          K1          2     0000   0000 0000 0010│
   │                                                                     │
   │                                                                     │
   │                                                                     │
   └───────────────────────────────────────────────────────────────────┘
```

4. Press <alt> s to obtain the Saved Setups window.
5. The display now becomes as shown below,

```
Working Area                  Offline    FLASH1                FX         Ladder
Find      Save    Name        Copy       Move      Delete      Exchange   Test
Step      I/o     Text
─────────────────────────────────────────────────────────────────────────────
                      ──────── Device Monitor ── Saved Setups ────────
   ┌──────────────────────────────────────────┬────────────┐
   │  I/O     Name    Decimal    Pre/ASC    He │    3210     │
   │  X0               1           ☺      ┌──────────┐ 1     │
   │  Y0               1           ☺      │ _        │ 1     │
   │  T0              10          K10     └──────────┘1010   │
   │  T1               2          K1        │    0010     │
   │                                        └────────────┘
   └──────────────────────────────────────────────────────┘
```

6. Enter flash1 as the name under which the monitor elements will be saved.

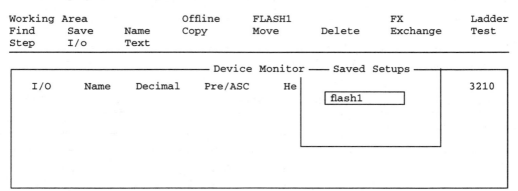

```
Working Area            Offline    FLASH1                    FX            Ladder
Find      Save   Name   Copy       Move        Delete        Exchange      Test
Step      I/o    Text
```
```
─────────────────────── Device Monitor ── Saved Setups ─
   I/O      Name    Decimal    Pre/ASC      He                         3210
   X0                 1           ☺             ┌─────────────────┐      1
                                                │ flash1          │
   Y0                 1           ☺             └─────────────────┘      1
   T0                 10         K10                                    1010
   T1                 2          K1                                     0010
```

7. Press <ent> for the monitor elements to be saved and for the setup window to be removed.

Recalling the saved elements

To recall the saved elements, which are to be monitored carry out the following:

1. Ensure the display is of FLASH1 in Device Mode, that is from the Ladder Menu enter:
   (a) F2
   (b) F9
2. Press <alt> r to obtain the Saved Setups window.
3. The display now becomes as shown below.

```
Working Area            Offline    FLASH1                    FX            Ladder
Find      Save   Name   Copy       Move        Delete        Exchange      Test
Step      I/o    Text
```
```
─────────────────────── Device Monitor ── Saved Setups ─
   I/O      Name    Decimal    Pre/ASC      He                         3210
                                                ┌─────────────────┐
                                                │ flash1          │
                                                └─────────────────┘
```

4. Ensure flash1 is highlighted within the name window and press <ent>.
5. The previously saved elements will now appear, whilst the Saved Setups window will disappear.
6. Press <F8> to enable Decimal Device Monitoring to recommence.

Note

1. *For each project, up to a maximum of 10 sets of monitored elements can be saved, with each set having its own setup name.*
2. *Use the vertical cursor keys to select which set of monitored elements is to be recalled.*
3. *On switching to monitoring using the ladder diagram, the recalled monitored elements can be used for monitoring purposes, by selecting the appropriate monitor page displayed at the bottom of the ladder diagram.*

8
PLC programs

To gain experience of using the MEDOC software and the FX PLC, a range of fairly simple programs will now be developed and tested. These PLC programs could be used to replace conventional systems consisting of relays, timers and counters. The following is a list of such programs which will be treated in turn in this chapter.

1. TRAF1   Traffic light controller
2. FURN1   Furnace temperature controller
3. INTLK1   Safety interlock circuit
4. LATCH1   Mains failure latch circuit
5. COUNT1   Extended time delay
6. COUNT2   On-line programming
7. BATCH1   Batch counter
8. COUNT3   Reversible up/down counter

8.1   Traffic light controller – TRAF1

Task

Using MEDOC produce a PLC ladder diagram which can enable an FX series PLC to simulate, a simple combinational logic traffic light controller.

Block diagram

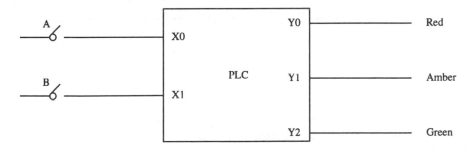

Determined by the condition of the input switches A and B, the output lights will turn ON/OFF according to the truth table below.

Note

- If the input switch or the output is OFF = logic 0.
- If the input switch or the output is ON = logic 1.

Truth table

Inputs		Outputs		
A (X0)	B (X1)	Red (Y0)	Amber (Y1)	Green (Y2)
0	0	1	0	0
0	1	1	1	0
1	0	0	0	1
1	1	0	1	0

Solution

By inspection it can be seen that

$$\text{Red} \ \ = \bar{A}$$
$$\text{Amber} = B$$
$$\text{Green} \ = A.\bar{B}$$

The above can be proved theoretically, using either Boolean algebra or Karnaugh mapping techniques.

PLC ladder diagram – TRAF1

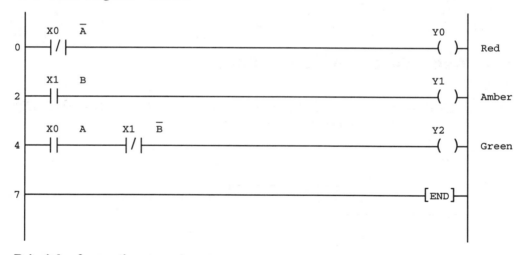

Principle of operation

1. Line 0
   When there is no input on X0 (i.e. A = 0), then the red output Y0 will be ON. Conversely, when A = 1, the red output will be OFF.
2. Line 2
   The B input X1 is directly connected to the amber output Y1, thus producing the truth table below.

B input (X1)	Amber output (Y1)
0	ON
1	OFF

3. Line 4

   To turn the green output Y2 ON, input A should be ON whilst input B should remain OFF.

8.2 Furnace temperature controller – FURN1

A furnace has to be controlled from cold between the limits of a low temperature setting t_l and an upper temperature setting t_u. The technique discussed here ensures that the furnace will not be turned ON/OFF as often as it would be if only a single thermostat were used. This ensures that the life of the electric elements within an electric furnace, will be extended. Similarly, in a gas-fired furnace the life of the gas burners would also be extended.

Block diagram

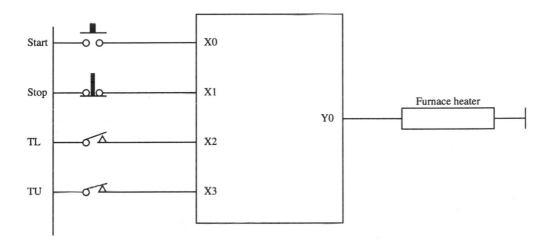

Description

Let T be the temperature of the furnace. Then, while heating,

$$
\begin{array}{ll}
t < t_l & \text{furnace ON} \\
t < t_u & \text{furnace ON} \\
t \geq t_u & \text{furnace OFF}
\end{array}
$$

and while cooling

$$
\begin{array}{ll}
t < t_u & \text{furnace OFF} \\
t \leq t_l & \text{furnace ON}
\end{array}
$$

Temperature response characteristic

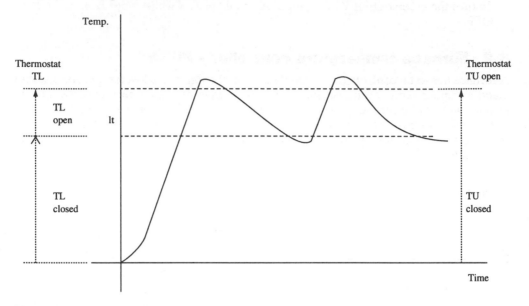

Temperature sensor TL

When the temperature of the furnace is below t_l, then the lower temperature sensor TL, will be closed. When the temperature of the furnace is equal to and above t_l, then the lower temperature sensor, TL, will be open

Temperature sensor TU

When the temperature of the furnace is below t_u, then the upper temperature sensor TU will be closed. When the temperature of the furnace is equal to and above t_u, the upper temperature sensor TU, will be open

Safety procedures

1. Thermostats are used whose contacts are closed when the temperature is below their set value. This ensures that if the connections to the thermostats or the thermostats themselves, become open circuit, the furnace will switch OFF, that is a fail safe condition.
2. Also for safety purposes, the stop button X1 must be normally closed. This ensures that if the wire connecting to the stop button breaks, the system will again fail safe. Hence, on the ladder diagram, the stop input is entered as a normally open contact.
3. For further details on safety see Chapter 10.

System algorithm

1. When the start button is operated and with both TL and TU closed, the furnace heater will turn ON.
2. When TL is opened and TU is still closed, the furnace heater will still remain ON.
3. When TU is opened, then the furnace heater will be turned OFF. This causes the furnace to cool down at its natural cooling rate.
4. When TL recloses, the furnace heater will again be turned ON.

Task

Design a PLC ladder diagram which will meet the requirements of the furnace control system.

Solution

Ladder diagram – FURN1

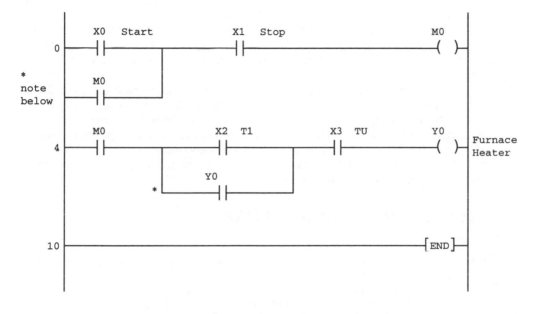

*Note

To enter M0 after all of line 0 has been entered, carry out the following:

1. *Place the write cursor below X0.*
2. *Enter 3 for a single, normally open, parallel contact.*
3. *Enter M0 <ent>.*
4. *Repeat the same procedure at line 4, that is complete the top rung and then under X2 enter:*
   (a) *3*   *for a single parallel contact.*
   (b) *Y0 <ent>*   *for the normally open contact Y0.*

Principle of operation

1. Line 0
   The normally open contact X0, the normally open contact X1, which is connected to the normally closed contacts of the stop button and the internal memory coil M0, form a start/stop latch circuit.
2. The operation of the start push button, X0, will cause M0 to energize and latch via its own contact.
3. Line 4
   When the furnace is cold, the thermostats TL and TU will be closed and therefore inputs X2 and X3 will be ON.

4. With the operation of X0 and thus the operation of M0, the circuit is complete and hence the output Y0 will turn ON.
5. With the operation of Y0, the furnace will now start to heat up.
6. When the furnace temperature reaches the lower temperature setting, then thermostat TL will open and therefore input X2 will be OFF, but since the contact Y0 is closed this will ensure that the output Y0 remains energized and hence the furnace will continue to heat up.
7. When the furnace temperature reaches the upper temperature setting, thermostat TU will open and therefore input X3 will also be OFF. This causes the Y0 latch circuit to be broken, which causes output Y0 to turn OFF.
8. As soon as the furnace cools down slightly, then the upper temperature thermostat will remake, causing input X3 to be ON. However, since the Y0 latch circuit has been broken, the output Y0 will not re-energize until input X2 is ON, that is when TL remakes.
9. The furnace now starts to cool down at its normal cooling rate until the lower temperature thermostat TL closes, causing Input X2 to turn ON and so enabling output Y0 to re-energize. This, in turn, causes the furnace to heat up again.
10. The furnace temperature will now be kept within the lower and upper temperature limits set by the thermostats TL and TU. When the stop push button, X1, is operated, the M0 latch circuit will be broken. This will cause the furnace to cool down completely to normal room temperature.

8.3 Safety interlock circuit – INTLK1

Description

An automatic sauce blending control system, which consists of three main sections, has also to be operated manually.

Section	Input (Manual)	Output
1. Hopper input	X0	Y0
2. Weigher output	X1	Y1
3. Blender output	X2	Y2

As part of the manual operation of the system, the inputs X0, X1 and X2 are connected to push buttons, to enable the following outputs Y0, Y1 and Y2 to be manually operated. However, it is an essential requirement of the design that an interlock circuit be included, which will ensure that only one of the Outputs can be ON at any one time.

Blending system diagram

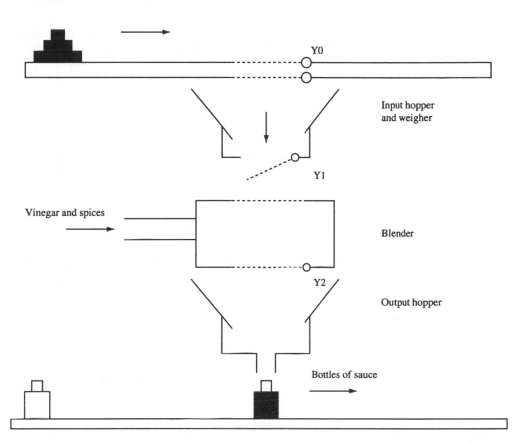

Tomatoes

Y0

Input hopper
and weigher

Y1

Vinegar and spices

Blender

Y2

Output hopper

Bottles of sauce

Task

Produce a PLC ladder diagram which ensures that only one of the output solenoids can be ON, at one time.

- X0 is a normally open push button which is used to energize and latch the hopper input solenoid Y0.
- X1 is a normally open push button which is used to energize and latch the hopper output solenoid Y1.
- X2 is a normally open push button which is used to energize and latch the blender output solenoid Y2.
- X3 is a normally closed push button/switch which is used to reset any latched output.

Solution

Ladder diagram – INTLK1

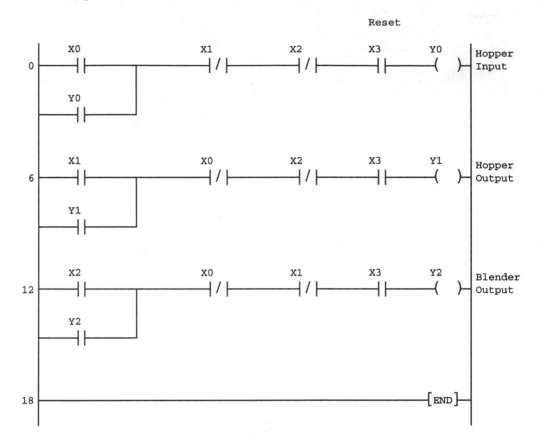

Principle of operation

1. Switch the reset, X3, ON.
2. The basic circuit consists of three latch circuits.
3. When any one of the inputs X0, X1, X2 is operated it will energize and latch its corresponding output solenoid.
4. At the same time, if there is another output which has been previously energized and latched, then the normally closed contact of the input, which has just operated, will break the latch to that particular output. Hence, only one output can be on, at any one time.
5. The operating of X3 will now enable the last output to have been latched to be deenergized.

8.4 Latch relays

Latch relays are used to ensure, that should there be an interruption in the voltage supply due either to a mains failure or to a fault in the dc power supply, it will still be possible for the program to continue execution from the point it was at when the interruption occurred.

The latch relays use battery backup to retain their ON/OFF condition, whenever there is an interruption to the voltage supply.

Latch memory range

The latch memory range on the FX PLC is M500–M1535.

Ladder diagram – LATCH1

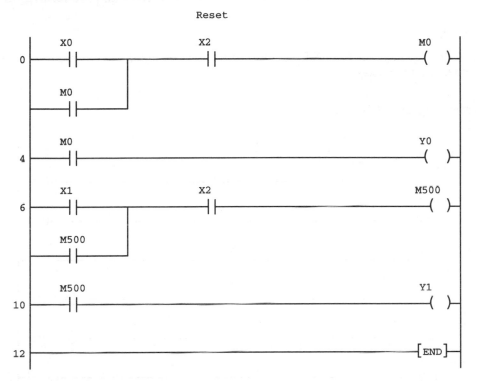

Principle of operation – LATCH1

1. Enter, test and save the project LATCH1.
2. Download the project to the FX PLC.
3. Ensure the project is working correctly using the inputs X0, X1 and X2.
4. Line 0
   Input X0 operates M0, which then latches via its own contact and also energizes output Y0.
5. Line 6
   Input X1 operates M500, which then latches via its own contact and also energizes output Y1.
6. Reset
   Opening input X2 resets both latch circuits, provided inputs X0 and X1 are OFF.
7. With input X2 ON, momentarily turn ON then OFF inputs X0 and X1, so that both outputs Y0 and Y1 are turned ON.
8. Momentarily turn OFF the 240 V mains supply to the FX PLC.
9. When the mains supply is turned back ON, only the Output Y1 will be ON, because the internal latch memory coil M500 will have battery backup.

8.5 Counters

Counters are very important parts of a sequence control system. They can be used for example:

1. To ensure that a particular part of a sequence is repeated a known number of times.
2. To count the number of items being loaded into a carton.
3. To count the number of items passing along a conveyor belt, in a given time.
4. To position a component. See Centring sysrem – CENTRE 1 on page 195.

COUNT1

The following example, COUNT1, demonstrates how a counter can be used to produce an extended time delay.

Ladder diagram – COUNT1

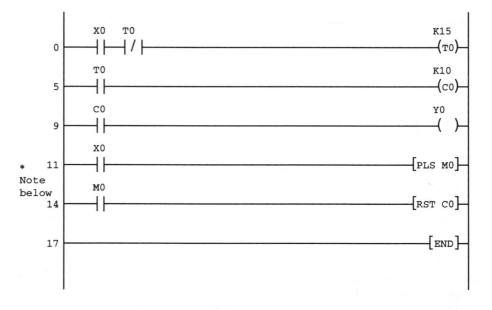

*Note
1. To enter –[PLS MO]– *enter the following:*
  (a) pls <ent>
  (b) m0 <ent>
2. Use the same procedure for –[RST CO]–*, that is*
  (a) rst <ent>
  (b) c0 <ent>

Principle of operation
1. Line 0
   The closing of input X0, and the normally closed timer contact T0, will provide a path to enable the coil of timer T0 to be energized.

After 1.5 seconds, timer T0 times out and its normally closed contact will open, causing the timer to become de-energized for a time equal to one scan time, which for COUNT1 will be approximately 1.5 milliseconds.

With the timer dropping out its contact recloses causing the timer to be re-energized once more.

This cut-throat timer circuit is effectively a pulse oscillator, whose contacts momentarily operate every 1.5 seconds.

2. Line 5

With the momentary closure of the normally open contacts of T0, a count pulse is sent to counter C0 every 1.5 seconds.

3. Line 9

Counter C0 counts the incoming pulses and when the number of pulses equals the preset K value (i.e. 10), all the C0 contacts operate as follows:

(a) All normally open contacts, close.

(b) All normally closed contacts, open.

The normally open contact C0 closes, hence energizing the output coil Y0.

Therefore, the circuit gives an output signal on Y0 15 seconds after the input X0 closes. Hence the circuit can be considered as an extended timer.

4. Line 11

On line 11, whenever input X0 closes, this energizes a special output, which is known as a pulse circuit, PLS.

A pulse circuit only operates on the closing of an input and when energized, the pulse circuit will cause its associated output, the internal memory M0, to energize for a time equal to one scan time for the program.

Hence the contacts of M0 will be closed for approximately 1.5 milliseconds.

5. Line 14

(a) PLS waveforms

The following are the waveforms associated with the PLS circuit:

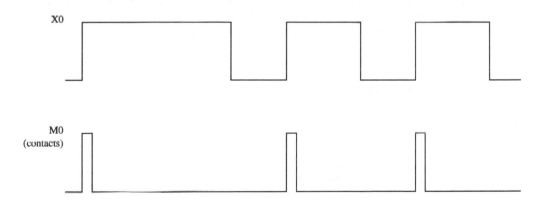

From these waveforms, it can be seen that each time input X0 operates, the instruction PLS M0 will be executed and the normally open contact of M0 will momentarily close, thus causing the counter C0 to be reset to zero.

(b) Hence with the operation of input X0 and the resetting of counter C0, the cycle will repeat itself.

(c) Even though input X0 remains closed, the pulse circuit will not reoperate until input X0 reopens and closes again.

Monitoring

Carry out the following:

1. Open a new project and give it the name COUNT1.
2. Enter the ladder diagram.
3. Test and save the program.
5. Download to the FX PLC.
6. Monitor the ladder diagram COUNT1, using the following function keys:
   (a) <F2>
   (b) <F8>
7. Note that:
   (a) At the bottom of the display both timer T0 and counter C0 are counting up.
   (b) When counter C0 reaches 10, then 15 seconds will have elapsed since input X0 was closed.

PLC version number

The next section describes the facility of on-line programming, that is how to modify a PLC program, whilst the PLC is in RUN. However, this facility was only introduced into FX PLCs from Version 2.0 onwards.

   The version number is stored in an internal data register D8001 and by monitoring the contents of this data register, it is possible to determine the version number of the PLC being used.

Note

Data registers are covered in Chapter 16.
To determine the version number of the PLC in use, carry out the following:

1. The project currently loaded into the PLC is COUNT1 and this will be used to demonstrate how the version number is obtained.
2. Ensure the ladder diagram COUNT1 is being displayed.
3. Monitor COUNT1 using:
   (a) <F2>
   (b) <F8>
4. Press <F5> to enter the Monitor Edit Mode.
5. Enter the following:
   (a) T0
   (b) T1
   (c) D8001
6. Press <F5> to return to Monitor Mode.
7. The display will now become as shown on the facing page.

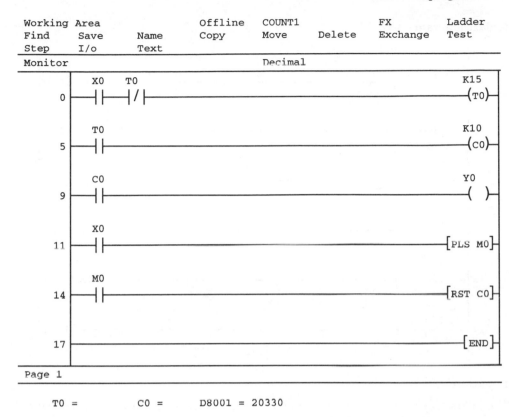

Working	Area		Offline	COUNT1		FX	Ladder
Find	Save	Name	Copy	Move	Delete	Exchange	Test
Step	I/o	Text					
Monitor				Decimal			

```
        X0    T0                                            K15
 0     ─┤├──┤/├─────────────────────────────────────────(T0)─

        T0                                                  K10
 5     ─┤├──────────────────────────────────────────────(C0)─

        C0                                                  Y0
 9     ─┤├──────────────────────────────────────────────( )─

        X0
11     ─┤├────────────────────────────────────────────[PLS M0]─

        M0
14     ─┤├────────────────────────────────────────────[RST C0]─


17     ──────────────────────────────────────────────────[END]─
```

Page 1

T0 =   C0 =   D8001 = 20330

Contents of D8001

The contents of D8001 are interpreted as follows.

$$2\;0\;3\;3\;0$$

| |
PLC   Version
type   number

1. The first number (i.e. 2) refers to the PLC type (i.e. an FX PLC).
2. The last three numbers refer to the version number (i.e. Version 3.30).
3. Hence, since this particular PLC is later than Version 2.0, it can be used for on-line programming.

8.6 On-line programming

Using the on-line programming facility of MEDOC, it is possible to modify one line at a time of the project, even though the PLC is in RUN.

In a continuous process, on-line programming can be dangerous, since once the modifications have been entered, they become operative on the next scan of the program.

The project COUNT2 is used to demonstrate the use of the on-line programming facility.

Using the method of copying as described on page 27, copy the project COUNT1 to COUNT2.

Ladder diagram – COUNT2

Procedure

The following procedure describes how the constant for counter C0, is changed from K10 to K20 using on-line programming.

1. Load the project COUNT2.
2. Ensure that the ladder diagram for the project COUNT2 is being displayed and the PLC is in RUN.
3. Enter the following:
   (a) <F2> to select the working area.
   (b) <alt> O to select the on-line facility.
4. If the following message appears

Invalid PLC type

---

check the version number as described on page 78 and verify the PLC is earlier than Version 2.0
5. If the PLC is Version 2.0 or later, then the display will become as shown on the facing page.

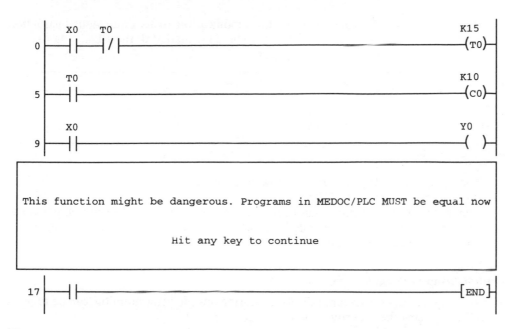

This function might be dangerous. Programs in MEDOC/PLC MUST be equal now

Hit any key to continue

Note

At the top of the diagram, Offline now changes to Online, and also flashes ON and OFF.

6. Using the vertical cursor keys move the cursor down to the start of line 5, where the element to be changed (i.e. the counter value of C0) is located.

7. Press <F7> for the write mode.

8. Note that only line 5 is now being displayed, with the write cursor situated at the start of line 5.
9. Move the write cursor one position to the right, so that it is on the right hand side of the T0 contact.
10. Enter the following:
    (a) 7 for an output coil.
    (b) C0 <ent>.
    (c) K20 <ent>.

11. Press <F7> for the conversion of the modification to its equivalent instruction program and for the modified program to be downloaded to the PLC.
The following message will now appear:

```
This function is dangerous are you sure Y/N? N
```
---

12. Press Y.
Note the short flashing message

```
Writing to PLC
```

The complete ladder diagram will now be displayed.
13. Press <esc> to return to Offline.
14. Check that the modification has been successfully carried out, by observing that the total time delay is now 30 seconds. That is, the time delay from input X0 being turned ON until the output Y0 turns ON is 30 seconds.

On-line programming, security messages

The security messages, which are displayed during on-line programming, can be toggled ON/OFF, by using the security option:

1. From the Main Menu, select Options.
2. Select Security.
3. The display now becomes as shown below.

```
Select function                        COUNT2      FX        Options
Attribut       Quiet        Security
Turn Security ON or OFF
```

```
Security is now ON
```
---

4. Press <ent> to toggle the security facility ON/OFF.

8.7 Practical BATCH1

Task

Design a batch counter program to carry out the following sequence:

1. Use input X0 to reset counter C0.
2. Use input X1 to input pulses to the counter.
3. After 10 input pulses, output Y0 is to come ON.
4. Resetting the counter will turn the output OFF and enable counting to be repeated.

Solution

Batch counter – BATCH1

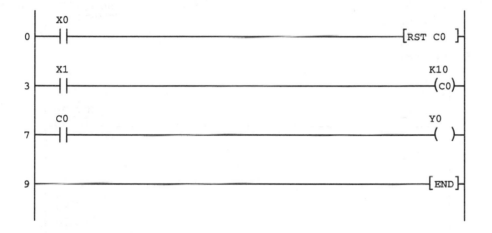

Principle of operation

1. Line 0
   The momentary operation of input X0 will reset the counter C0. This, in turn, will cause output Y0 to turn OFF (line 8).
2. Line 3
   Each time input X1 closes, this will increment the contents of C0.
3. Line 7
   After input X1 has been pulsed 10 times, the C0 contacts will operate, to energize output Y0.

8.8   Bi-directional counters

There are many applications in PLC control systems where the positioning of a component is done by counting pulses from a datum point. This could be required, for example, where the positioning of the component is done using a conveyor system driven by a stepper motor.

When the stepper motor is pulsed forward in a clockwise direction, the same pulses would be used to increment the counter, and when the stepper motor is pulsed in the anti-clockwise direction, the pulses would be used to decrement the counter.

COUNT3

The following program, COUNT3, uses the bi-directional counters C200 and C201 and their associated special memory coils M8200 and M8201, which enables the counters to count either up or down.

Counter C200 is set to a positive value (i.e. K10) and C201 is set to a negative value (i.e. K – 10).

Ladder diagram – COUNT3

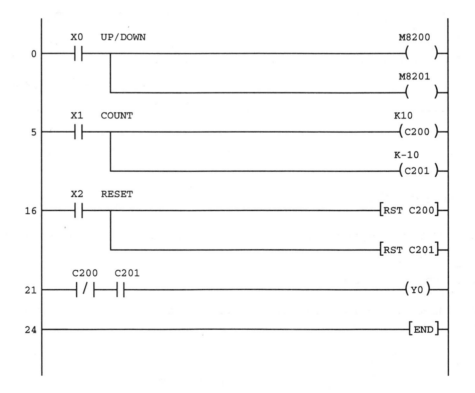

Special memory coils M8200–M8234

The special memory coils M8200–M8234 are only used in conjunction with the bi-directional counters C200–C234 respectively. Each of these special memory coils controls whether or not its associated bi-directional counter, will count up or count down.

	Special memory coil	Associated bi-directional counter
M8200–M8234 off then C200–C234 count up	M8200	C200
	M8201	C201
	M8201	C201
	M8201	C201
M8200–M8234 on then C200–C234 count down	M8201	C201
	M8201	C201
	M8201	C201
	M8201	C201
	M8234	C234

Principle of operation – COUNT3

1. Line 0
   (a) Input X0 operates the special memory coils M8200 and M8201.
   (b) When M8200 and M8201 are not operated, the counters C200 and C201, will count up.
   (c) Conversely, when M8200 andM8201 are operated, then the counters C200 and C201 will count down.
2. Line 5
   The pulsing of input X1 will simutaneously increment/decrement both counters C200 and C201. Input X0, determining the direction of the count.
3. Line 16
   The operation of input X2 will reset both counters to zero.
4. Lines 0 and 5
   (a) Initially operate input X0 and by pulsing input X1, decrement both counters to −15.
   (b) Open input X1, so that both counters can now be incremented.
   (c) Pulse input X1 to increment both counters to +11.
5. The following observations will now be found:
   (a) Incrementing count
       When incrementing the count:
       C201 will turn ON when the count goes from −11 to −10.
       C200 will turn ON when the count goes from +9 to +10.
   (b) Decrementing count
       When decrementing the count:
       C200 will turn OFF when the count goes from +10 to +9.
       C201 will turn OFF when the count goes from −10 to −11.
6. Line 21
   The output Y0 will be ON while the count is in the range −10 to +9.

9
Sequence controller

The following notes describe how a system which consists of two pneumatic pistons can be controlled using a Mitsubishi FX PLC.

The PLC is required to operate two single-acting electrically actuated pneumatic pilot valves, which in turn control the two pneumatic pistons.

Basic system

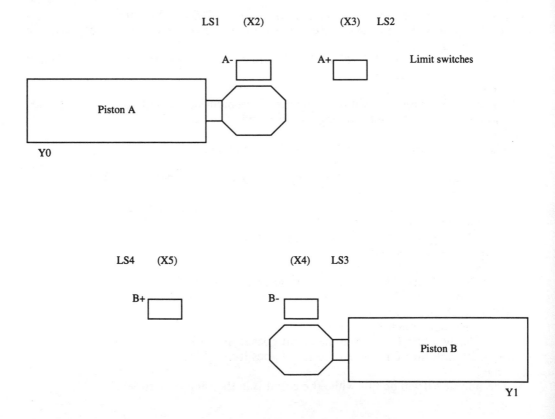

LS1–LS4 Limit switches

Sequence of operation

The sequence of operations for the two pistons is as follows:

1. Start of sequence
2. A+   Piston A out
3. B+   Piston B out
4. A–   Piston A in
5. 5 second time delay
6. B–   Piston B in
7. End of sequence

9.1 Sequence function chart

A sequence function chart (SFC) is a pictorial representation of a system's individual operations which, when combined, shows the complete sequence of events. Once this diagram has been produced, the corresponding ladder diagram can be more easily designed from it.

There is now software, one version being CADEPA, which enables the user to enter the program in SFC form and then the SFC is converted to the ladder diagram for the PLC being used. The CADEPA software can be used with the majority of PLCs available.

For further information on the CADEPA software contact

FAMIC Ltd
2 The Chase
Fox Holes Business Park
Hertford, Hertfordshire
SG13 7NN
UK

Sequence function chart – PNEU1

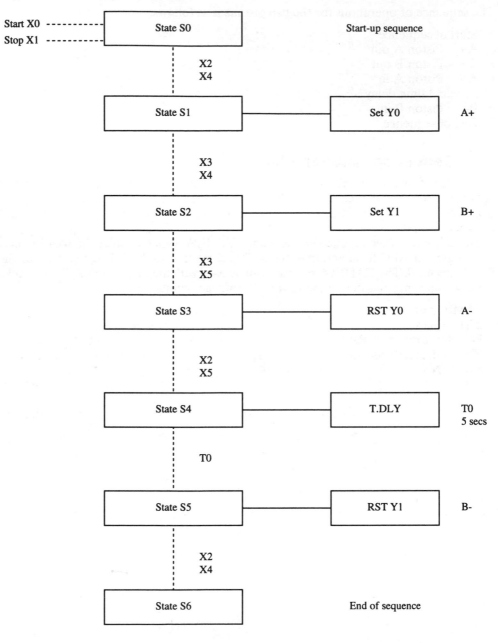

Description – SFC

1. The SFC consists basically of a number of separate sequentially connected states, which are the individual constituents of the complete machine cycle, which controls the system. An analogy is that each state is like a piece of a jigsaw puzzle: on its own it does not show very much, but when all the pieces are correctly assembled then the complete picture is revealed.
   Each state has the following:
   (a) An input condition.
   (b) An output condition.
   (c) A transfer condition.
   When the input condition into a state is correct, then that state will produce an output condition. That is, an output device or devices will be:
   (a) Either turned ON and remain ON.
   (b) Or turned OFF and remain OFF.
2. When the output or outputs are turned ON/OFF, then the system's input conditions will change to produce a transfer condition.
3. The transfer condition is now connected to the input condition of the next sequential state.
4. If the new input condition is correct, then the sequence moves to the next state.
5. From the SFC for PNEU1, it can be seen that when the start push button is operated, this is the input condition for state 0.
6. The output condition from state 0 is the start-up sequence which will reset both solenoid A and solenoid B.
   With inputs X2 and X4 now made, the transfer from state 0 can take place.
7. The transfer conditions from state 0 are the correct input conditions for state 1. Hence the process now moves from state 0 to state 1.
8. The process will continue from one state to the next, until the complete machine cycle is complete.
9. From the SFC, the ladder diagram can now be produced either by the programmer or, if the SFC software is available, by using the computer to carry out the conversion process.

9.2 Ladder diagram – PNEU1

It will now be found that the production of the PLC ladder diagram from the SFC will be a far easier process.

PLC ladder diagram – PNEU1

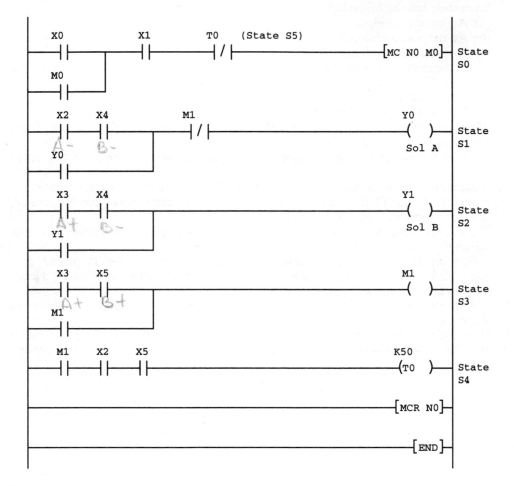

Note

The master contacts are entered as follows:

–[MC N0 M0]–	–[MCR N0]–
(a) mc \<ent\>	(a) mcr \<ent\>
(b) n0 \<ent\>	(b) n0 \<ent\>
(c) m0 \<ent\>	

Converted ladder diagram – PNEU1

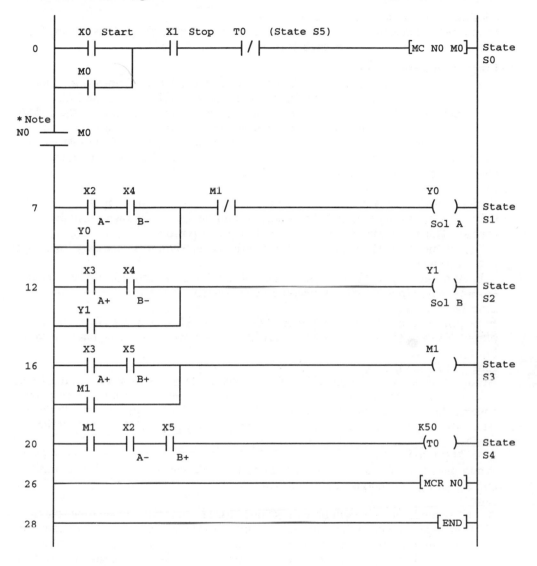

*Note

The serial master contacts NO ╪ MO *cannot be programmed in directly; they appear automatically when the ladder diagram is converted using <F7>, after the instruction* −[MC NO MO]−.

Principle of operation – single cycle

The following describes single-cycle operation.

The terms 'piston A operates' or 'piston B operates' refers to the pistons moving from their back positions A– or B– to their forward positions A+ or B+.

1. Line 0 (State S0)

   When input X0 is operated, this will cause the Master Control instruction –[MC N0 M0]– to be executed. This instruction is described later on page 172.

   Basically the Master Control instruction enables a particular part of the ladder diagram to become operative. This is shown on the ladder diagram as a pair of normally open horizontal contacts, which enables the operation of the instructions from lines 7 to 26. If the –[MC N0 M0]– instruction has not been executed, then the instructions from lines 7 to 26 will be ignored.

2. Line 7 (State S1)

   With pistons A and B in the back position (i.e. A– and B–), then inputs X2 and X4 will operate, causing output Y0 to energize and latch over its own normally open contact. This will cause piston A to move to the A+ position.

   The memory coil M1 will operate later in the cycle, when it is necessary for piston A to become de-energized.

   Even though input X2 now opens when piston A moves forward, the latch circuit ensures that output Y0 will not become de-energized.

3. Line 12 (State S2)

   With piston A fully forward, input X3 will operate. This, plus X4 (B–), will cause output Y1 to be energized and latch over its own contact. Piston B will now move to the B+ position.

4. Line 16 (State S3)

   At this moment, both pistons will be fully forward and hence inputs X3 and X4 will be operated. This will cause the memory coil M1 to operate and latch over its own contact. The normally closed contact of M1 at line 7 will now open and break the Y0 latch circuit. This will de-energize Y0 and hence cause piston A to retract to the A– position.

5. Line 20 (State S4)

   When piston A returns to the A– position, input X2 will remake and this, plus M1 and X5 (B+), will energize the timer coil T0.

6. Line 0

   After 5 seconds, timer T0 will time out (State S5). The normally closed timer contacts of T0 will open, breaking the start latch circuit. This will cause the master contact M0 to open, causing all of the energized outputs from lines 7 to 20 to become de-energized. Hence M1 will become de-energized, as will output Y1. The de-energizing of output Y1 will cause piston B to retract to the B– position.

7. Line 26

   The instruction –[MCR N0]– is used reset the Master Control instruction. Therefore the Master Control contacts will have no effect on any additional instructions following line 26.

9.3 Simulation – PNEU1

Using the switch box, simulate and monitor the operation of the pneumatic pistons A and B.

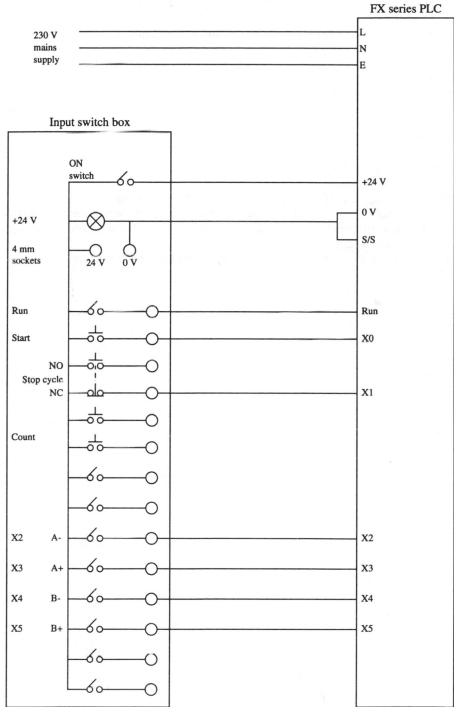

Simulation and monitoring procedure

1. **Display and monitor the ladder diagram PNEU1.**
2. **Operate the input switches X2 and X4.**
3. This will simulate the operation of the A– and B– limit switches.
4. **Press the start push button.**
5. Output Y0 will now be energized and this will cause piston A to operate to the A+ position.
6. In a real situation with piston A moving forward, its limit switches X2 would open and X3 would close.
7. **Open X2 and close X3.**
8. This will cause output Y1 to energize and hence enable piston B to move forward to its B+ position.
9. **Open X4 and close X5.**
10. Auxiliary output M1 will energise and cause output Y0 to de-energize. Hence Piston A will return to its A– position.
11. **Open X3 and close X4.**
12. With X2 closing, this will start the operation of the timer T0.
13. After 5 seconds, timer T0 will time out and its normally closed contact (Line 0), will open, breaking the master contact circuit of M0. Output Y1 will now be de-energized.
14. **OPEN X5 and close X2.**
15. The process can now be repeated, by pressing the start push button.

9.4 Pneumatic panel operation

The PLC can now be connected to a pneumatic panel, to enable the complete system to be tested. This enables the PLC and the program PNEU1 to control more of an industrial-type process, than just being simulated with switches and LEDs. The panel which has been used successfully for this purpose is produced by FESTO Ltd.

Pneumatic drawing – PNEU1

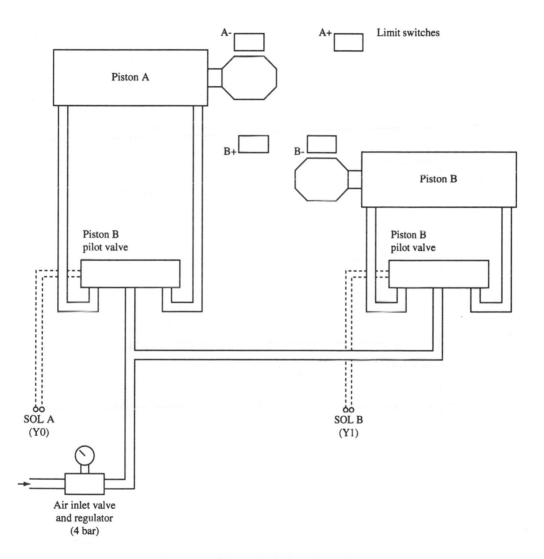

PNEU1 wiring diagram (relay output)

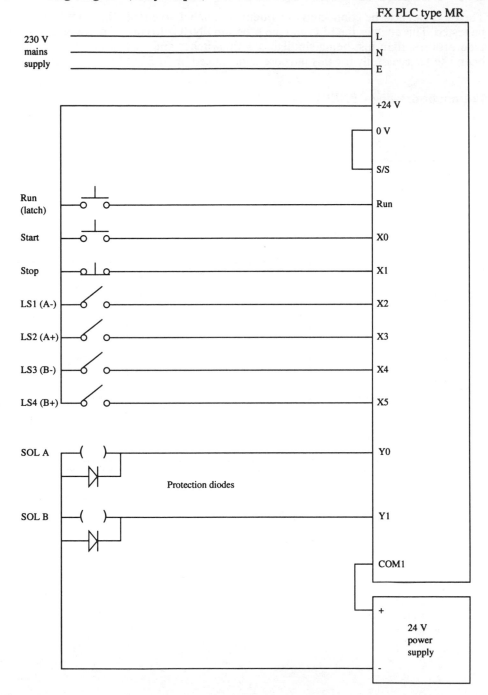

Note

An external power supply must be used to supply the output solenoids, as the PLC dc power supply is limited to 250 mA for the FX16–FX32 range and 400 mA for the FX48–FX60 range.

PNEU1 wiring diagram (transistor output)

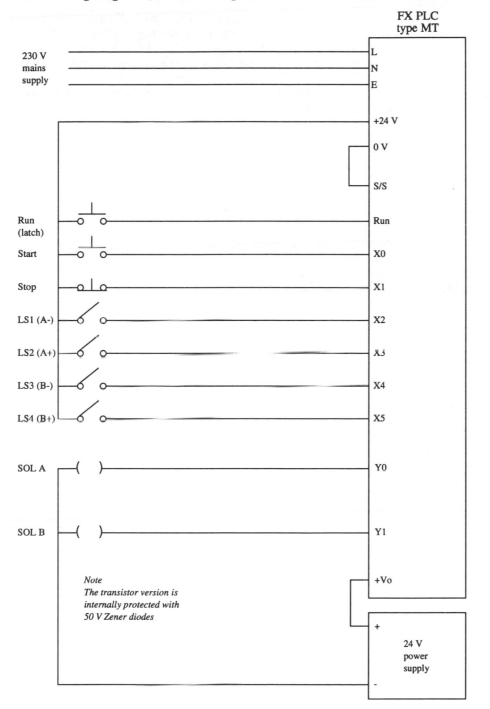

Note
*The transistor version is
internally protected with
50 V Zener diodes*

9.5 Forced input/output

The Mitsubishi FX PLC allows inputs and outputs to be turned ON and OFF directly from the computer. This is extremely useful when commisioning a system or when fault finding, because it enables a check to be carried out on the wiring from the inputs and outputs to the PLC and also determines whether or not the input and output devices are operating correctly.

The following describes how this facility can be used with the project PNEU1 whilst the PLC is still wired to the pneumatic panel.

Forcing the start input X0

1. Ensure that the ladder diagram PNEU1 is being displayed and that it has been downloaded to the PLC.
2. Turn the PLC RUN to ON.
3. Press the following:
   (a) <F2> to enter the working area.
       <ALT> H to obtain the condensed display.
   (b) <F8> to monitor.
   (c) <F7> to obtain the Forced I/O facility.
4. The display now appears as shown below.

Ladder diagram – PNEU1

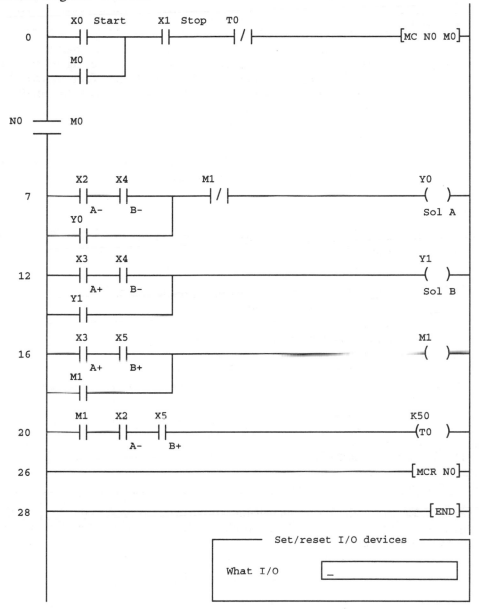

5. Within the Set/Reset window insert X0 <ent>.
6. The window now becomes

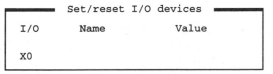

7. Press the <space> bar.

8. The following message now appears

```
This function may be dangerous. Are you sure Y/N? N
```
---

9. Press Y for yes and pistons A and B will go through one complete single cycle.
10. The monitor display of PNEU1 will not show X0 operating. The forcing of any input (i.e. X0) will only last for one scan time, as X0 will by turned OFF by the PLC program. The PLC program resets the condition of the forced input to the condition of the actual input.

Forcing the Y outputs

The Y outputs (i.e. Y0 and Y1) can also be forced ON/OFF. However as the PLC will override any forced output, it is necessary before forcing outputs to turn the PLC RUN to OFF.

Forcing the output Y0

1. Ensure that the ladder diagram PNEU1 is being displayed and that it has been downloaded to the PLC.
2. Turn the PLC RUN to OFF
3. Press the following:
   (a) <F2> to enter the working area (ignore if already done).
   (b) <F8> to monitor (ignore if already done).
   (c) <F7> to obtain the Forced I/O facility.
4. Within the Set/Reset window insert Y0 <ent>.
5. The window now becomes

```
━━━━━━━━━━  Set/reset I/O devices  ━━━━━
  I/O        Name           Value

  Y0
```

6. Press the <space> bar.
7. The following message now appears:

```
This function may be dangerous. Are you sure (Y/N)? N
```
---

8. Press Y for yes and the Y0 output will energize to drive piston A to the A+ position.
9. Also the Set/Reset window will now display a box under value, indicating that the output Y0 has been turned ON:

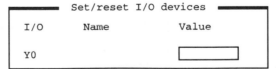

10. Repeat the process to turn Y0 OFF by pressing:
    (a) The <space> bar.
    (b) The 'Y'button.
11. Press <F7>, and this time enter Y1 <ent>.
12. Repeat the procedure by pressing the <space> bar and the 'Y' button, so that the output Y1 can now be forced ON/OFF.
13. Before quitting the Forced I/O facility ensure that no outputs have been left forced ON.
14. Press <esc> to return to monitor mode.

10
Safety

In any industrial design safety must be a first priority, in that the designer(s) must take **all** reasonable steps to ensure a person or persons cannot be harmed in any way whilst the system is being operated.

There are now European Machinery Safety Standards, which also include the control systems of the machinery. These can be summarized as follows:

1. All emergency circuits such as emergency stop buttons and safety guard switches must be hard wired and not depend on software, that is PLCs or electronic logic gates.
2. A designer(s) must carry out a risk assessment procedure. In addition the procedure must be documented for possible inspection at any time.
3. Any changes to the design must be implemented as far as possible to limit any risk.
4. Where there are remaining risks, then the use of safeguards must be implemented into the design.

For further details on safety, the following booklet is recommended as essential: *A Guide to European Machinery Safety Standards* published by

PILZ UK
Willow House
Medlicott Close
Oakley Hay Business Park
Corby, Northants
NN18 9NF
UK

10.1   **Emergency stop requirements** (reference diagram page 103)

An emergency stop circuit must meet the following requirements:

1. It is independent of software and digital logic circuits.
2. The emergency stop button should be wired to a safety relay circuit, that is one in which the relays use positive guidance contacts.
   See item 5 below.
3. It must have inbuilt redundancy, that is more than one safety relay (e.g. R1 and R2).

Note

The coils of R1 and R2 are connected in parallel, whilst their contacts are connected in series.

4. It must have a cross-check circuit (i.e. R3) which checks whether R1 or R2 is stuck in the closed position.
5. By using positive guidance contacts, it should check whether any contacts have become welded together, owing to a high current passing through them whilst closed. The positive guidance contacts ensure that none of the normally closed contacts can reclose, if any of the normally open contacts have become welded together.
6. A mains failure facility which ensures that, if there is a mains failure, the outputs cannot be automatically re-energized when the mains supply is restored.

10.2 PNEU1 wiring diagram – emergency stop circuit

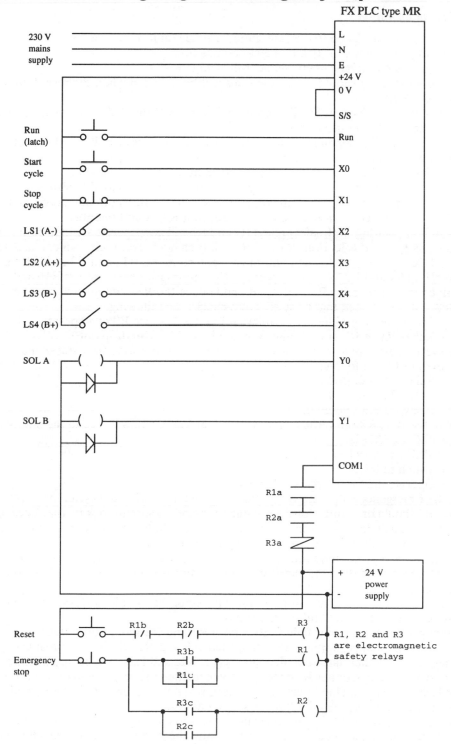

10.3 Emergency stop circuit

Principle of operation

1. This circuit is designed to operate should a single fault occur, that is:
   (a) Only one relay will stick in the closed position.
   (b) Only one normally open contact will weld closed.
   (c) If either fault should occur, then this will be detected when the reset button is operated.
2. Switch the PLC RUN OFF. This ensures that none of the PLC outputs can be ON.
3. Operate the Reset push button.
4. Relay R3 will now operate via the normally closed contacts of R1b and R2b provided the following has not occurred:
   (a) Neither safety relay R1 nor R2 has stuck in the closed position.
   (b) None of the R1 and R2 normally open contacts have welded together.
   Either of the faults (a) or (b) will prevent the R1b or the R2b normally closed contacts being able to reclose and hence this ensures that R3 cannot operate.
5. With R3 operating, both safety relays R1 and R2 will now operate via their respective contacts R3b and R3c. Both R1 and R2 will then latch over their own contacts R1c and R2c respectively. Also, the normally open contacts, R1a and R2a will close.
6. As relays R1 and R2 have now operated, their normally open contacts R1b and R2b will open causing relay R3 to drop out and hence the R3a contact will remake.
7. Hence it can be seen that relay R3 cross-checks the following:
   (a) There are no problems with relays R1 and R2 before R3 can operate.
   (b) Either R1 or R2 or both must operate before R3 can drop out.
8. However, before power can be connected to the PLC outputs, the states of the safety relays must be as follows:
   (a) Relay R1 operated.
   (b) Relay R2 operated.
   (c) Relay R3 not operated.
   With the R1a, R2a and R3a contacts closed, power can now be fed to the outputs of the PLC via COM1.
9. The PLC can now be operated:
   (a) Switch to RUN.
   (b) Operate the Start Cycle push button.
10. If the Emergency Stop button is pressed at any time during the cycle, then both R1 and R2 should drop out. However, if one of the relays should stick in, then since this is only a single fault, the other relay will still be able to drop out and hence break the power supply circuit to the PLC outputs via COM1.
    Similarly, it is assumed that only one of the contacts (i.e. R1a or R2a) will weld together, even if the same level of fault current is flowing through these series-connected contacts.
    Hence if the emergency stop button is pressed, the circuit to COM1 can still be broken when relays R1 and/or R2 drop out.
11. Finally if there is a mains failure, then both R1 and R2 should drop out.
    When the mains supply is restored, then R1 and R2 will not automatically re-energize, since their latch circuit contacts (i.e. R1c and R2c) will be open. However, if one of the relays, either R1 or R2 has stuck in, then the respective contact (i.e.R1b or R2b) will not be able to close. Therefore when the mains supply is restored and the reset button is pressed, relay R3 will not energize.
12. Hence power to the PLC outputs cannot be restored until the reset button is pressed and the safety circuits have been automatically checked and found to be all right.

11
Documentation

The documentation of a ladder diagram is an essential part of the design process, in that without good documentation, those people who are responsible for maintaining any system controlled by a PLC will have great difficulty in understanding how the system operates.

There are three ways in which a PLC ladder diagram can be documented. These are:

1. Comments.
2. Element names.
3. Header information.

11.1 Comments

A ladder diagram can be commented by inserting lines of text, for example:

1. At the start of the program to describe its overall purpose.
2. At selected points within the program, for instance at the start of a section dealing with analogue-to-digital conversion.

The following enables a brief description of the project PNEU1 to be inserted at the start of the ladder diagram.

1. Display the ladder diagram of PNEU1.
2. Press <F2> to enter the working area.
3. Position the cursor at the start of line 0.
4. Press <F5>. A small white square, the comment cursor, now appears above line 0.
5. Enter PNEU1 <ent>.
6. As soon as the first letter is entered, the square is immediately replaced with a rectangular window, into which the remainder of the comment is entered.
7. The comment cursor now moves down to the next line.
8. Enter the second comment, control of pneumatic System <ent>.
9. To insert a blank line enter <ent>.
10. To quit the comment mode, press <F5>.
11. The display now becomes as shown overleaf.

106 *Programmable Logic Controllers*

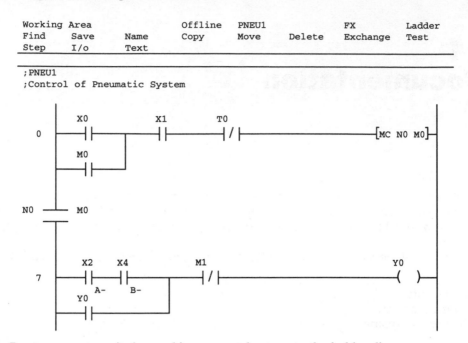

;PNEU1
;Control of Pneumatic System

12. Press <esc> to quit the working area and return to the ladder diagram menu.

Deleting a comment

To delete a comment place the small green cursor on the comment line which is to be deleted and press <F6>.

11.2 Name list editor

The second method for documenting a ladder diagram i.e. PNEU1, is to allocate to each PLC element a meaningful name.

   When required, the ladder diagram can be displayed with both the comments and the names. For example, the information on the diagram below indicates more clearly the function of the circuit (it is a latching start/stop circuit).

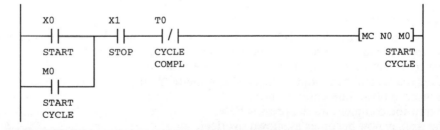

The following describes how the name list editor is used:

1. It will be assumed that the project PNEU1 has been loaded and the Main Menu is being displayed.
2. Select Edit.
3. From the edit menu, select Name.

4. Press <F2> to enter the Working area.
5. Press <F5> to enter the Name List Editor. Toggling <F5> will cause entry/exit from the editor.
6. If the following names, including spaces, are entered in blocks of five characters, the names will be displayed much neater on the ladder diagram.
7. The display will now be as shown below.

```
Working Area                               PNEU1    FX       Name
   Find      Save      Copy    Move   Delete   Exchange  Test
   I/o       Name      Text
─────────────────────────────────────────────────────────────────
   Press F5 to end insert
─────────────────────────────────────────────────────────────────

        I/O       Name            Comment              Remark


  ⇒ [        ]
```

The following information will now be entered:

(a)   X0 <ent> START <ent>   Start auto sequence <ent>   Page 1 <ent>
(b)   *Press <F10> if the next I/O number directly follows on*
      Else enter the required I/O number from the keyboard
(c)   X1   STOP   Stop auto sequence   Page 1 <ent>
(d)   X2   A–   Piston A limit switch LS1   <ent>
(e)   X3   A+   Piston A LS2   <ent>
(f)   X4   B–   Piston B LS3
(g)   X5   B+   Piston B LS4
(h)   Y0   SOL A   Piston A output solenoid
(i)   Y1   SOL B   Piston B output solenoid
(j)   M0   STARTCYCLE   Start single cycle   (Note block of
                                                        five characters)
(k)   M1   MEM LATCH   De-energize piston A   (Note block of
                                                        five characters)
(l)   T0   CYCLECOMPL   After 5 seconds, B–

8. Press <F5> to end insert.
9. Press <F2> to return to the Name Menu.
10. Select Test, to check for valid I/O numbers. This would be particularly useful where there is a change of PLC type.
11. Select Save, to save the names list.

Name list modifications

Modifications to the name list can be carried out by selecting Name from the Edit Menu.

1. To modify a name line:
   (a) Use the cursor keys to select the required line.
   (b) Press <ent> and insert required modifications.
2. To insert an additional name line:
   (a) Use the cursor keys to select where the insertion is required.
   (b) Press <F5> to enter the Name List Editor. A window will now appear in the I/O column, where the new name line is required.
   (c) Insert required details.
   (d) Press <F5> to quit the Name List Editor.
3. To remove an unwanted name line:
   (a) Press <F2> to obtain the cursor ⇒.

(b) Use the cursor keys to select the unwanted name line.
(d) Press <F6> to delete the unwanted line.
(e) Press <esc> and carry out the test and save procedures.

Display annotated ladder diagram

To display the annotated ladder diagram PNEU1, carry out the following:

1. Display the ladder diagram PNEU1.
2. Press <F2> to enter the working area.
3. Press <F4> to obtain the annotated ladder diagram.
4. Toggling <F4>, will cause the annotations to be either displayed or removed.

Annotated ladder diagram

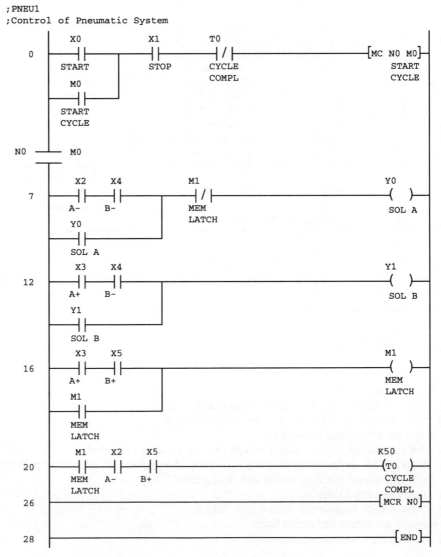

11.3 Name list – ladder menu

To check quickly whether or not an I/O name is included in the name list, while a ladder diagram is being displayed, carry out the following:

1. From the Ladder Menu select Name. Note this is not the same Name function which is obtained from the Edit Menu.
2. A large red window now appears on the right hand side of the display.
3. A message asks 'What I/O:'
4. Enter, for example, X0 <ent>.
5. Displayed in the window will now be a list of 16 inputs from X0 to X17 in octal, which are overlaid on top of the ladder diagram. The asterisk indicates the element is being used.

	Used	I/O	Name
⇒	*	X0	START
	*	X1	STOP
	*	X2	A–
	*	X3	A+
	*	X4	B–
	*	X5	B+
		X6	
		X7	
		X10	
		X11	
		X12	
		X13	
		X14	
		X15	
		X16	
		X17	

6. Press <esc> to remove the Name List window.

Adding a name to the Name List

To add a name to the Name List, while a ladder diagram is being displayed, carry out the following:

1. While the Name List window is displayed, use the cursor keys to select the required I/O.
2. Press <ent>.
3. Enter the required list in the Name column at the required I/O.
4. It is not possible to remove a name from the Name List, while in ladder mode. This can only be done while in the main Name List Editor, as described starting on page 106.

11.4 Name list – entry monitoring

Using the Name List display in ladder mode, it is possible to monitor the operation of the system.

1. From ladder mode select Name.
2. In the message window enter X0 <ent>.
3. The Name List window is now displayed overlaid on top of the ladder diagram.
4. Move the cursor down to X6, which is the first input X element not being used in PNEU1.
5. Press <F9>. The inputs X6 to X17, which are not being used, will now disappear.
6. Enter the remaining elements of PNEU1.

Note

It is not necessary to enter the assigned names, as they appear automatically after each element has been entered.

7. Enter
   (a) Y0 <ent>
   (b) Y1 <ent>
   (c) M0 <ent>
   (d) M1 <ent>
   (e) T0 <ent>

```
┌──────────────── Entry Monitor ────────────────┐
│                                                │
│       Used      I/O      Name                  │
│       *         X0       START                 │
│       *         X1       STOP                  │
│       *         X2       A-                    │
│       *         X3       A+                    │
│       *         X4       B-                    │
│       *         X5       B+                    │
│       *         Y0       SOL A                 │
│       *         Y1       SOL B                 │
│       *         M0       STARTCYCLE            │
│       *         M1       MEM LATCH             │
│       *         T0       CYCLECOMPL            │
└────────────────────────────────────────────────┘
```

8. Press <F8> to monitor the operation of PNEU1, using the entry monitor.

11.5   Header selection

The header enables additional information to be included with every page of the printout.

Header editor

1. From the Edit Menu select Header.
2. Press F2 to obtain the first edit window.
3. The display now becomes as shown below.

```
Working Area              PNEU1            FX            Header
Save      Copy
Save current header on disk
─────────────────────────────────────────────────────────────
```

```
┌───────────────────┬────────────┬──────────────┬──────────────┐
│ ┌───────────────┐ │            │ Date:        │ Proj: PNEU1  │
│ │ _             │ │            │              │              │
│ └───────────────┘ │            ├──────────────┼──────────────┤
│                   │            │ Rev. dat:    │ Syst: FX     │
│                   │            │              │              │
│                   │            ├──────────────┼──────────────┤
│                   │            │ Rev. no:     │ Type:        │
│                   │            │              │              │
│                   ├────────────┼──────────────┼──────────────┤
│                   │ Draw. no:  │ Sign:        │ Page:        │
└───────────────────┴────────────┴──────────────┴──────────────┘
```

4. Enter the required information shown below. Press <ent> to obtain each separate window in turn.

Pneumatic Control System	Ridley Eng. Ltd.	Date: 20/1/96	Proj: PNEU1
		Rev. dat:	Syst: FX
		Rev. no:	Type:
	Draw. no: 12345	Sign:	Page:

5. Press <esc> to quit the header editor.

12
Printouts

A very useful facility of MEDOC is that it can output a ladder diagram to a printer, to enable a 'hard' copy of the diagram to be obtained. In addition a printout can be obtained of all those elements which have been used, plus a cross-reference to those elements. It is also possible to save the ladder diagram to disk as a separate file, so that the ladder diagram can be imported into a word processor package. This procedure is described in section 12.2.

To obtain a printout of the ladder diagram plus its associated elements, carry out the following:

1. Ensure a parallel drive printer is connected to the computer.
2. From the main menu, select print. The VDU screen now becomes:

```
Select function                        PNEU1           FX         Print
Listings    I/o_Sel    Header    Go    Save    Recall  Default    Options
Select what listings you want to print and start with GO
```

List type	Step range	Start page	I/O type	I/O range
Text		1	Input	X0 - X177
Only Com	0 - 1999	1	Output	Y0 - Y177
Name		1	Mem/Latch	M0 - M8255
Instr	0 - 1999	1	LinkRel	
Ladder	0 - 1999	1	Timer	T0 - T255
Raw Ladder	0 - 1999	1	Counter	C0 - C255
Used I/o		1	DiagMem	
Crossref		1	State	S0 - S999
Parameter		1	DataReg	D0 - D8255
Basic		1	LinkReg	
DWR		1		
		Pointer	P0 - P63	
		Interrupt	I0 - I8	

```
    Print header at bottom
```

12.1 Printer setups

Before any printouts can be obtained, it is necessary to select the required printer setups. This ensures that only the required information is printed out and also that the MEDOC software is compatible with the printer being used.

Listings

Select the required list types, that is those items which, if they were all printed out, would provide the full documentation for the project.

1. Initially all of the list types, except for basic, are highlighted within a green window.
2. Select Listings <ent>.
3. A cursor ⇒ will now appear against the first item (i.e. Text).
4. Only the following four list types will initially be selected, for printout purposes:

| Name |

| Ladder |

| Used I/O |

| Crossref |

5. Use the vertical cursor keys to select each item in turn.
6. Toggling the <space> bar will turn the selected item ON/OFF.
7. Ensure that the four list types shown above are the only ones which remain highlighted.
8. The display should now be as shown below.

```
Select function                    PNEU1          FX          Print
Listings    I/o_Sel    Header    Go    Save    Recall   Default    Options
Select what listings you want to print and start with GO
```

List type	Step range	Start page	I/O type	I/O range
Text		1	Input	X0 – X177
Only Com	0 – 1999	1	Output	Y0 – Y177
Name		1	Mem/Latch	M0 – M8255
Instr	0 – 1999	1	LinkRel	
Ladder	0 – 1999	1	Timer	T0 – T255
Raw Ladder	0 – 1999	1	Counter	C0 – C255
Used I/o		1	DiagMem	
Crossref		1	State	S0 – S999
Parameter		1	DataReg	D0 – D8255
Basic		1	LinkReg	
DWR		1		
			Pointer	P0 – P63
			Interrupt	I0 – I8

```
Print header at bottom
```

9. Press <esc> to return to the Print Menu.

Input/output selection

1. To select the types and range of I/O which are to be printed out, select I/o_sel from the Print Menu.
2. The following notes describe how a particular I/O type can be selected for printing and how the I/O range of the selected type, can be changed to the range shown overleaf.

	I/O Type	I/O Range
	Input	X0 - X7
	Output	Y0 - Y7
	Mem/Latch	M0 - M7
	Timer	T0 - T7
	Counter	C0 - C7

3. Using the vertical cursor key, select each I/O types in turn.
4. If the selected I/O type is not to be printed out, press the <space> bar. The highlighting for those I/O types which are not being printed out must be OFF.
5. If the selected I/O type is to be printed out, then carry out the following:
   (a) Press the <space> bar to turn the highlighting OFF.
   (b) Press the <ent> key.
   This will turn the highlighting back ON and also display a window within which, the I/O Range can be changed.
6. Change the I/O range values to those shown on the previous page.
   Do not include the I/O type, that is X for input, Y for output, M for an auxiliary memory coil, etc. These will be automatically inserted, when the next item is carried out.
7. Press <ent> for the following to occur:
   (a) The I/O type (i.e. X, Y, M, etc.) will now be automatically inserted.
   (b) The cursor will move down to the next I/O type.
8. Press <esc> to return to the Print Menu.
9. The Print Menu should now be as shown below.

```
Select function                        PNEU1           FX          Print
Listings    I/o_Sel     Header    Go   Save   Recall   Default     Options
Select what listings you want to print and start with GO
```

List type	Step range	Start page	I/O type	I/O range
Text		1	Input	X0 - X7
Only Com	0 - 1999	1	Output	Y0 - Y7
Name		1	Mem/Latch	M0 - M7
Instr	0 - 1999	1	LinkRel	
Ladder	0 - 1999	1	Timer	T0 - T7
Raw Ladder	0 - 1999	1	Counter	C0 - C7
Used I/o		1	DiagMem	
Crossref		1	State	S0 - S999
Parameter		1	DataReg	D0 - D8255
Basic		1	LinkReg	
DWR		1		
			Pointer	P0 - P63
			Interrupt	I0 - I8

Print header at bottom

Header selection

The header, as mentioned previously, enables additional information to be included with each page of the printout.

The header selection covers the following:

1. The size of the header.
2. Page position, that is top or bottom of each page.
3. No header at all to be printed out.

The header selection is made as follows:

1. From the Print Menu select Header.
2. Press <ent> repeatedly until the message at the bottom of the VDU screen is

---

```
Print small header at top
```

12.2 Printout procedure

1. The Print Menu should now be as shown below.

```
Select function                          PNEU1              FX          Print
Listings     I/o_Sel     Header     Go    Save    Recall    Default     Options
Select what listings you want to print and start with GO
```

List type	Step range	Start page	I/O type	I/O range
Text		1	Input	X0 - X7
Only Com	0 - 1999	1	Output	Y0 - Y7
Name		1	Mem/Latch	M0 - M7
Instr	0 - 1999	1	LinkRel	
Ladder	0 - 1999	1	Timer	T0 - T7
Raw Ladder	0 - 1999	1	Counter	C0 - C7
Used I/o		1	DiagMem	
Crossref		1	State	S0 - S999
Parameter		1	DataReg	D0 - D8255
Basic		1	LinkReg	
DWR		1		
			Pointer	P0 - P63
			Interrupt	I0 - I8

```
   Print small header at top
```

2. Select Save to save the print requirements.

Printer setup menu

Before obtaining a printout, it is necessary to check the Printer Setup Menu. This must be done to ensure that:

1. A blank sheet of paper is not being printed out after each page of information.
2. The ladder diagram will consist of straight lines and not small circles.

Printer options

1. From the Print Menu select Options.
2. From the Options Menu select Printer.
3. Ensure the display is as shown below.

```
Select function                                    PNEU1      FX      Options
Line      New_Page      Printer      Output       Save
Select printer settings
```

```
                          Printer Setting
          ⇒   Interface         Parallel 1
              Bit rate          2400
              Word length       8
              Parity            None

              Format length     11¨       (Prevents blank sheets)
              Line space        1/6¨
              Character set      English (Ensures straight lines)

              Start sequence
              End sequence
```

Changing the printer options

To change the format length and the character set, carry out the following:

1. Ensure that the double cursor ⇒ is displayed.
2. Move the cursor down to Format length.
3. Press the <ent> key until the Format length is 11″.
4. Move the cursor down to Character set.
5. Press the <ent> key until the Character set becomes English.
6. Press <esc> to return to the Options Menu and select Save.
7. This will save the selected printer settings to disk.

Obtaining a printout

Finally, to obtain the required printouts, carry out the following:

1. Press <esc> to return to the Print Menu.
2. Select Go.

PNEU1 printouts

Name

I/O	Name	Comment	Remark
X0	START	Start auto sequence	Page 1
X1	STOP	Stop auto sequence	Page 1
X2	A−	Piston A limit switch LS1	
X3	A+	Piston A LS2	
X4	B−	Piston B LS3	
X5	B+	Piston B LS4	
Y0	SOL A	Piston A output solenoid	
Y1	SOL B	Piston B output solenoid	
M0	STARTCYCLE	Start single cycle	
M1	MEM LATCH	De-energize piston A	
T0	CYCLECOMPL	After 5 seconds B−	

Ladder diagram – PNEU1

;PNEU1
;Control of Pneumatic System

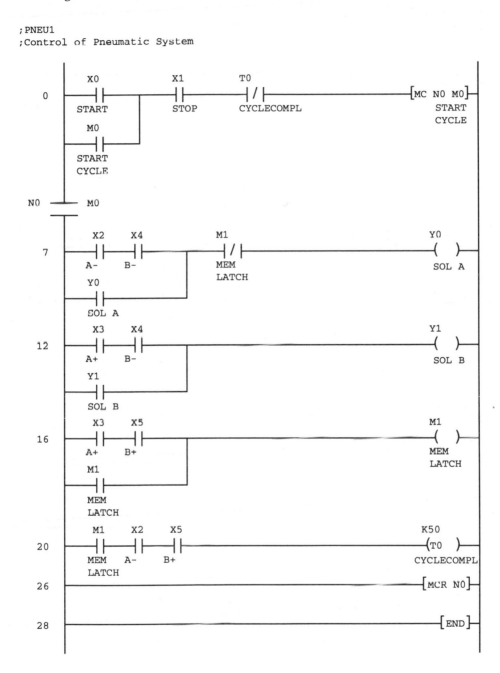

Used I/O
The asterisk (*) indicates:

1. Used contact I I.
2. Used coil ( ).

──────────────────────────── Input ────────────────────────────

	II	( )			II	( )			II	( )			II	( )
X0	*	–	X1		*	–	X2		*	–	X3		*	–
X4	*	–	X5		*	–	X6		–	–	X7		–	–

──────────────────────────── Output ────────────────────────────

	II	( )			II	( )			II	( )			II	( )
Y0	*	*	Y1		*	*	Y2		–	–	Y3		–	–
Y4	–	–	Y5		–	–	Y6		–	–	Y7		–	–

──────────────────────────── Mem/Latch ────────────────────────────

	II	( )			II	( )			II	( )			II	( )
M0	*	*	M1		*	*	M2		–	–	M3		–	–
M4	–	–	M5		–	–	M6		–	–	M7		–	–

──────────────────────────── Timer ────────────────────────────

	II	( )			II	( )			II	( )			II	( )
T0	*	*	T1		–	–	T2		–	–	T3		–	–
T4	–	–	T5		–	–	T6		–	–	T7		–	–

──────────────────────────── Counter ────────────────────────────

	II	( )			II	( )			II	( )			II	( )
C0	–	–	C1		–	–	C2		–	–	C3		–	–
C4	–	–	C5		–	–	C6		–	–	C7		–	–

* = used   E0 = Dual coil   E1 = No coil   E2 = No contact   E3 = SET/RST no match

For further details on these error codes refer to page 121.

Cross-reference
The cross-reference list gives the step numbers of all the elements being used in the program. This enables both a coil and all its contacts to be easily located on the ladder diagram printout.
For example, consider memory coil M1.

1. Step 10   normally closed contact.
2. Step 18   normally open contact.
3. Step 19   coil.
4. Step 20   normally open contact

```
──────────────────────────── Input ────────────────────────────
   X0              START              Start auto sequence              Page 1
           0        -II-
   X1              STOP               Stop auto sequence               Page 1
           2        -II-
   X2              A-                 Piston A limit switch LS1
           7        -II-      21       -II-
   X3              A+                 Piston A LS2
          12        -II-      16       -II-
   X4              B-                 Piston B LS3
           8        -II-      13       -II-
   X5              B+                 Piston B LS4
          17        -II-      22       -II-

──────────────────────────── Output ───────────────────────────
   Y0              SOL A              Piston A output solenoid
           9        -II-      11      -( )-
   Y1              SOL B              Piston B output solenoid
          14        -II-      15      -( )-

─────────────────────────── Mem/Latch ─────────────────────────
   M0              STARTCYCLE         Start single cycle
           1        -II-       4      [MC]
   M1              MEM LATCH          De-energize piston A
          10        -I/I-     18       -II-        19    -( )-    20    -II-

──────────────────────────── Timer ────────────────────────────
   T0              CYCLECOMPL         After 5 seconds, B-
           3        -II-      23      -( )-
```

12.3 Printing to a file

The information which is sent to a printer can instead be sent to a file and stored in the sub-directory currently being used (i.e. c:\medoc\trg). The file is a simple text file and if required can be imported into a word processor package, where it can be edited.

1. From the Print Menu select Options.
2. The display becomes as shown below.

```
Select function                                    PNEU1      FX       Options
Line        New_Page        Printer      Output    Save
Select printer settings
```
___

```
                              Printer Setting

                    Interface          Parallel  1
                    Bit rate           2400
                    Word length        8
                    Parity             None
                    Format length      11"
                    Line space         1/6"
                    Character set       English
                    Start sequence
                    End sequence
```

3. Select Output.

```
Select function                                    PNEU1      FX       Options
Line        New_Page        Printer      Output    Save
Select printer settings
```
___

```
                              Printer Setting

                    Interface          File: [ _        ]
                    Bit rate           2400
                    Word length        8
                    Parity             None
                    Format length      11"
                    Line space         1/6"
                    Character set       English
                    Start sequence
                    End sequence
```

4. Within the window enter the filename, pneu1 <ent>.
5. The file now becomes PNEU1.TMP.
6. Select Save to save the printer settings.
7. Press <esc> to return to the Print Menu and select Go.
8. Press <ent> to confirm that only one copy is required.
9. The following message is now displayed:

___
```
Printing will be directed to PNEU1.TMP Continue (Y/N)? N
```
___

10. Press Y to confirm that the information is to be directed to the file PNEU1.TMP in the sub-directory c:/medoc/trg.
11. This file can now be displayed on the VDU by carrying out the following:
    (a) Quit MEDOC.
    (b) Wait for the DOS prompt c:\medoc.
    (c) Enter the following:

    type c:\medoc\trg\pneu1.tmp ¦ more

12. Press the <space> bar to view the next page.
13. Alternatively, to view and also edit the file, use the DOS® EDIT facility.

12.4 Used I/O error codes

In a large program, especially one that has been extensively modified, it is possible that the following mistakes may occur. For example:

1. An output is used more than once.
2. Contacts are used for which there is no output.
3. An output is used, but without any contacts.
4. A set instruction is used, but without the corresponding reset.

Unfortunately none of these errors are reported when a Test on the ladder diagram is carried out.

The following ladder diagram ERROR1, contains all of the above errors and will be used to obtain the used I/O error codes.

Enter the ladder diagram ERROR1 and confirm that the Test option does not report any errors.

Ladder diagram – ERROR1

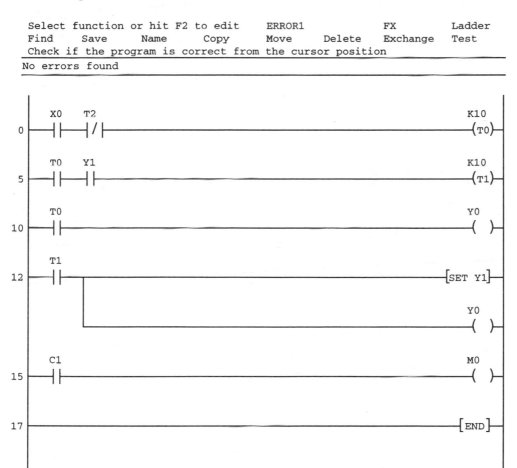

```
Select function or hit F2 to edit     ERROR1           FX        Ladder
Find      Save      Name      Copy     Move     Delete   Exchange  Test
Check if the program is correct from the cursor position
No errors found
```

Obtaining a printout

To obtain a printout of the ladder diagram ERROR1, carry out the following:

1. Select Print and modify the Print Setup Menu until it is as shown below.

```
Select function                        ERROR1              FX          Print
Listings    I/o_Sel    Header    Go    Save      Recall    Default     Options
Select what listings you want to print and start with GOS
```

List type	Step range	Start page	I/O Type	I/O range
Text		1	Input	X0 - X7
Only Com	0 - 1999	1	Output	Y0 - Y7
Name		1	Mem/Latch	M0 - M7
Instr	0 - 1999	1	LinkRel	
Ladder	0 - 1999	1	Timer	T0 - T7
Raw Ladder	0 - 1999	1	Counter	C0 - C7
Used I/o		1	DiagMem	
Crossref		1	State	S0 - S999
Parameter		1	DataReg	D0 - D8255
Basic		1	LinkReg	
DWR		1		
			Pointer	P0 - P63
			Interrupt	I0 - I8

```
Print without header
```

2. Select Save.
3. Ensure the picture options are as shown on page 178.
4. Select Go to obtain the raw ladder diagram and the used I/O, printouts.

Used I/O

──────────────────────────── Input ────────────────────────────

	I	I	( )		I	I	( )		I	I	( )		I	I	( )
X0	*	-		X1	-	-		X2	-	-		X3	-	-	
X4	-	-		X5	-	-		X6	-	-		X7	-	-	

──────────────────────────── Output ────────────────────────────

	I	I	( )		I	I	( )		I	I	( )		I	I	( )
Y0	-	*	E0	Y1	*	*	E3	Y2	-	-		Y3	-	-	
Y4	-	-		Y5	-	-		Y6	-	-		Y7	-	-	

──────────────────────────── Mem/Latch ────────────────────────────

	I	I	( )		I	I	( )		I	I	( )		I	I	( )
M0	*	*	E2	M1	-	-		M2	-	-		M3	-	-	
M4	-	-		M5	-	-		M6	-	-		M7	-	-	

──────────────────────────── Timer ────────────────────────────

	I	I	( )		I	I	( )		I	I	( )		I	I	( )
T0	*	*		T1	*	*		T2	*	-	E1	T3	-	-	
T4	-	-		T5	-	-		T6	-	-		T7	-	-	

──────────────────────────── Counter ────────────────────────────

	I	I	( )		I	I	( )		I	I	( )		I	I	( )
C0	-	-		C1	*	-	E1	C2	-	-		C3	-	-	
C4	-	-		C5	-	-		C6	-	-		C7	-	-	

* = used   E0 = Dual coil   E1 = No coil   E2 = No contact   E3 = SET/RST no match

Explanation – used I/O error codes

Refer to the diagram as shown on page 123.
1. Line 0

```
T2 E1 - No Coil
```

There is a normally closed contact of timer T2, but there is no T2 timer coil.
2. Lines 10 and 12

```
Y0 E0 - Dual coil
```

The output coil Y0 is used more than once.
3. Line 12

```
Y1 E3 - SET/RST no match
```

The set instruction (i.e. SET Y1) is used, but there is no corresponding RST Y1 instruction.
4. Line 15

```
C1 E1 - No coil
```

There is a normally open contact of counter C1, but there is no C1 counter coil.
5. Line 15

```
M0 E2 - No contact
```

There is an output M0, but no contacts of M0 are being used.

13
Files

The files option in the MEDOC software enables copies of any project to be copied:

1. To the same sub-directory, but with a different project name.
2. To a different sub-directory with the same name or with a different name.
3. To a $3^1/_2$ inch disk in the A drive.

In an industrial situation, it is essential that backup copies of all PLC projects are made. This ensures that if by mistake an existing PLC program is accidentally erased by transferring a different project or by transferring an earlier version of the project to a PLC, then there will always be a copy of the project on disk, which is available to ensure production can be maintained.

To be absolutely safe, copies of all projects should be saved on $3^1/_2$ inch disks, and held as follows:

1. A working copy held by the Maintenance Department.
2. A backup copy held by the Production Engineering Department.
3. A master copy held in the company safe.

The following describes how backup copies of projects are obtained:

1. From the Main Menu, select Files.
2. The display now becomes as shown below.

```
Select Function                                                    Files
Listproj    Dir_Set    Copy     Erase    Rename    Save    Quick   Format
List current directory
_____

            ┌─────────────────────────────────────────────┐
            │           MELSEC  M E D O C                   │
            │                                               │
            │     Programming and Documentation System      │
            │     for all Programmable Controllers from     │
            │                                               │
            │     M i t s u b i s h i E l e c t r i c       │
            │                                               │
            │              Version 1.64b                    │
            │     WORCESTER COLLEGE OF TECH. No 2790        │
            │                                               │
            │   Copyright (c) 1990, 1991, 1992, 1993, 1994  │
            └─────────────────────────────────────────────┘

     Use cursor keys to select and then press ENTER or enter 1st letter
```

3. Insert a $3^1/_2$ inch high density disk into the A drive of the computer.
4. If the disk has not been formatted, then select Format from the Files Menu and carry out the format instructions as they are displayed on the VDU.

13.1 Saving projects on the A drive

To select the A drive for saving the project files, carry out the following:

1. Ensure there is a formatted 3½ inch disk in the A drive.
2. From the Files Menu, select Dir_Set.
3. The display will now become as shown below.

```
Select function                                               Files
ListProj    Dir_Set    Copy     Erase    Rename    Save    Quick    Format
Select source disk and directory
```

```
Enter new directory:  | C:\MEDOC\TRG                            |

Directories under C:\MEDOC

LIST OF C:\MEDOC              <DIR>     DATE      TIME
DIRECTORIES
```

4. Within the new directory window, use the <space> bar to delete the existing directory (i.e. C:\MEDOC\TRG).
5. Enter a:\fx <ent>.
   The following message is now displayed:

```
Directory doesn't exist. Create directory (Y/N)? Y
```
---

6. Press <ent> to enable the sub-directory FX to be created.
7. The message now changes to

```
Do you wish to save directory setting (Y?N) ? Y
```
---

8. Press <ent>.

This will ensure that all future projects, or copies of existing PLC projects, will be saved on the A drive disk, in the sub-directory FX.

13.2 Copying a project to the A drive

To copy a project from the C drive to a 3½ inch disk in the A drive, carry out the following:

1. Ensure there is a formatted 3½ inch disk in the A drive.
2. From the Main Menu, select Files.
3. Enter Dir_Set.
4. Ensure the directory is C:\MEDOC\TRG.
5. Press <esc> and select Copy.
6. The display will now become as shown overleaf.

```
Select function                                                      Files
ListProj    Dir_Set     Copy      Erase     Rename    Save    Quick   Format
Select source disk and directory
```

Select a project with the cursor keys and ENTER. Turn page with PgUp and PgDn

PROJECT	PLC-type	Steps	Size	Name	Instr	Date	Time
FLASH1	FX	12	4232	TEST	TEST	2-12-95	14:15
FLASH2	FX	12	4232	TEST	TEST	2-12-95	16:50
FLASH3	FX						
FLASH4	FX						
TEST1	F1/F2						
TRAF1	FX						
FURN1	FX						
INTLK1	FX			**Project details**			
LATCH1	FX						
COUNT1	FX						
COUNT2	FX						
BATCH1	FX						
PNEU1	FX						
ERROR1	FX						

7. Use the vertical cursor key to select PNEU1.
8. The display will now become as shown below.

```
Select function                                                      Files
ListProj    Dir_Set     Copy      Erase     Rename    Save    Quick   Format
Select source disk and directory
```

Enter name of copy: | PNEU1 |

PROJECT	PLC-type	Steps	Size	Name	Instr	Date	Time
FLASH1	FX	12	4232	TEST	TEST	2-12-95	14:15
FLASH2	FX	12	4232	TEST	TEST	2-12-95	16:50
FLASH3	FX						
FLASH4	FX						
TEST1	F1/F2						
TRAF1	FX						
FURN1	FX						
INTLK1	FX			**Project details**			
LATCH1	FX						
COUNT1	FX						
COUNT2	FX						
BATCH1	FX						
PNEU1	FX						
ERROR1	FX						

9. Since the project name PNEU1 is not being changed, press <ent>.
10. Change the destination drive and path to a:\fx.
11. The displayed messages are now as follows:

```
Select function                                                      Files
ListProj    Dir_Set     Copy      Erase     Rename    Save    Quick   Format
Select source disk and directory
```

```
Enter name of copy: PNEU1
Enter destination drive and path:  | a:\fx                              |
```

12. Press <ent>.
13. The displayed messages now become

```
Select function                                              Files
ListProj    Dir_Set     Copy     Erase     Rename    Save    Quick    Format
Select source disk and directory
```
```
Make sure the right diskettes are mounted. Hit ENTER to continue
```

```
Enter name of copy: PNEU1
Enter destination drive and path: a:\fx
```

14. Press <ent> and the project PNEU1 will be copied to the $3^1/_2$ inch disk in the A drive.
15. Press <esc> to return to the Main Menu.

13.3 Sub-directory listing

When a new session of MEDOC is started and Files is selected, then by default, the last directory which had been saved is displayed. However, also by default, the directories under C:\MEDOC are also displayed.

If just a listing of the projects which have been saved on the A drive is required, carry out the following:

1. Insert the $3^1/_2$ inch disk, which is to be checked into the A drive.
2. From the Files Menu select Dir_Set.
3. Enter a:\.
5. Press <F8>.
6. A list of all the sub-directories on the A drive disk will now be displayed.

```
Select function                                              Files
ListProj    Dir_Set     Copy     Erase     Rename    Save    Quick    Format
Select source disk and directory
```
```
Enter new directory:  [ A:\                                        ]

Directories under A:\

LIST OF A DRIVE              <DIR>     DATE      TIME
DIRECTORIES
```

7. Pressing <F7> and entering a file specification (i.e. a:\fx*.prg <ent>) will enable a complete listing of all of the projects in the a:\fx sub-directory to be obtained.
8. Hit any key to continue.
9. If any of these existing projects are to be opened, it will be necessary first of all to change the directory setting to a:\fx and press <ent>.

Note

Pressing <F9> will enable the previously used sub-directory to be obtained.

Special purpose M coils

Within the PLC there are a group of special M coils starting at M8000. These special coils can be used in programs to provide information such as when the PLC is switched to RUN, timing signals, multi-mode operation, error reporting, etc. The list below contains just some of the coils which are available and which are used in this book. For a complete list, consult the Mitsubishi FX Programming Manual.

- M8000   These contacts are continuously closed whilst the PLC is in RUN.
- M8002   A one-shot pulse whose contacts close for just one scan time, when the PLC RUN input is operated.
- M8011   0.01 second pulses: 0.005 seconds ON, 0.005 seconds OFF.
- M8012   0.1 second pulses: 0.05 seconds ON, 0.05 seconds OFF.
- M8013   1.0 second pulses: 0.5 seconds ON, 0.5 seconds OFF.
- M8022   Carry used with arithmetic and shift instructions.
- M8041   Transfer used in multi-mode programs.
- M8044   Zero position used in multi-mode programs.
- M8067   Error used with binary-coded decimal numbers.
- M8200–M8234   Used for bi-directional counting.

14
Step ladder programming

Step ladder programming is an extension to conventional ladder programming, which enables the easier programming of continuous, sequential PLC control systems. It is only available on the F and FX series of Mitsubishi PLCs, and not on the A series.

The complete process is broken down into a number of discrete steps, each step containing the instructions required for just that particular area (step) of the program. For example, if during an automatic cycle the Stop Cycle button is operated, the operation will still continue until the end of the complete cycle. The program, on returning back to the first step, will then stop.

14.1 State memories (S)

The PLC elements, which enable control to be transferred from one state to the next, are known as state memories and their associated normally open contacts as STL. The basic principle underlying step ladder programming, is that there can only be one STL contact ON at any one time.

There are five types of state memories, as listed below, some of which will be used later in the step ladder project PNEU2 and the multi-sequence project PNEU3.

Address range – state memory coils

- Initial state   S0–S9   (10)   Used at the start of a step ladder program.
- Zero return   S10–S19   (10)   Used when a process is to be automatically returned to its start position.
- General use   S20–S499   (480)
- Retention   S500–S899   (400)
  (battery backed)
- Annunciator   S900–S999   (100)   Used with the annunciator-ANS
  (battery backed)   instruction

Note

The following notes apply to the use of state memory coils:

1. *Where step ladder programming is not being used, S coils can be used in the same manner as auxiliary M coils.*
2. *An STL instruction cannot be used in interrupt or sub-routine programs.*
3. *A master contact MC instruction cannot be used in an STL circuit.*
4. *When transferring from one state to a distant (i.e. non-consecutive) state, then an Out instruction (i.e. —( )—) is used instead of the Set instruction.*

14.2 PNEU2 (step ladder programming)

The program PNEU2 carries out the same sequence of operations as PNEU1, but unlike PNEU1, which used a standard ladder diagram, PNEU2 uses step ladder programming techniques.

Basic system

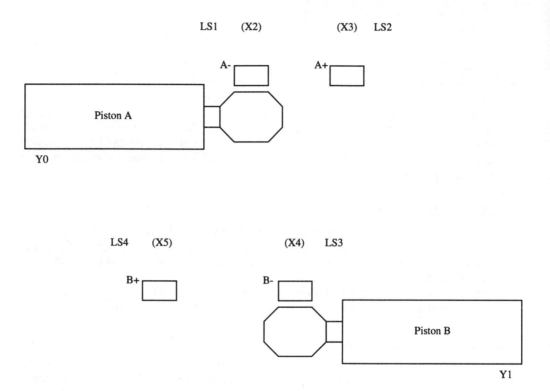

Sequence of operation – automatic cycle

The sequence of operations for the two pistons is as follows:

1. Press start.
2. A+   Piston A out
3. B+   Piston B out
4. A−   Piston A in
5. 5 second time delay.
6. B−   Piston B in
7. Repeat sequence.

14.3   Sequence function chart – PNEU2

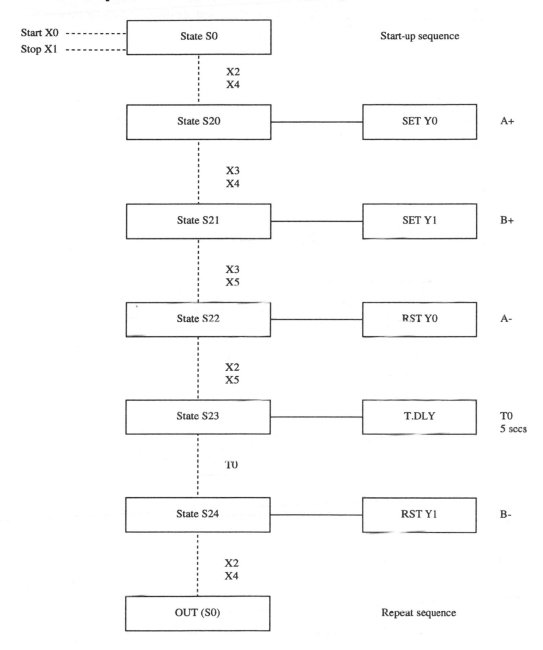

See note 4 on page 129, concerning the instruction OUT(S0).

Note

The sequence function chart is similar to the one shown on page 88, except that the state numbers correspond to the actual S coil numbers.

14.4 Step ladder diagram – PNEU2

From the sequential function chart, the following step ladder diagram can be produced.

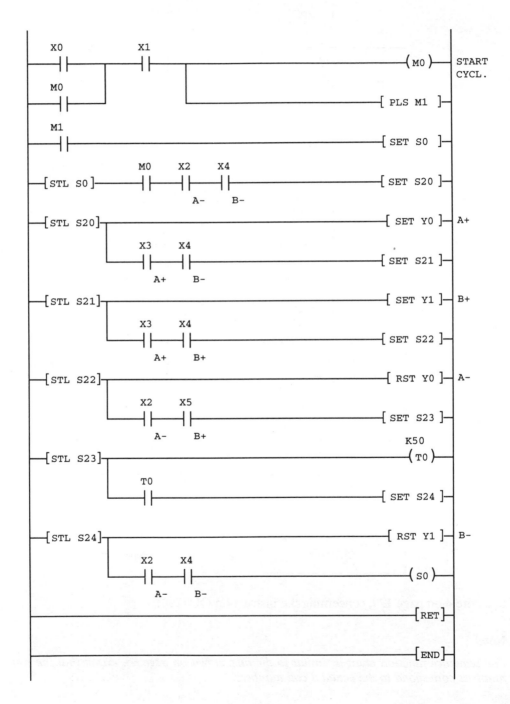

Converted step ladder diagram – PNEU2

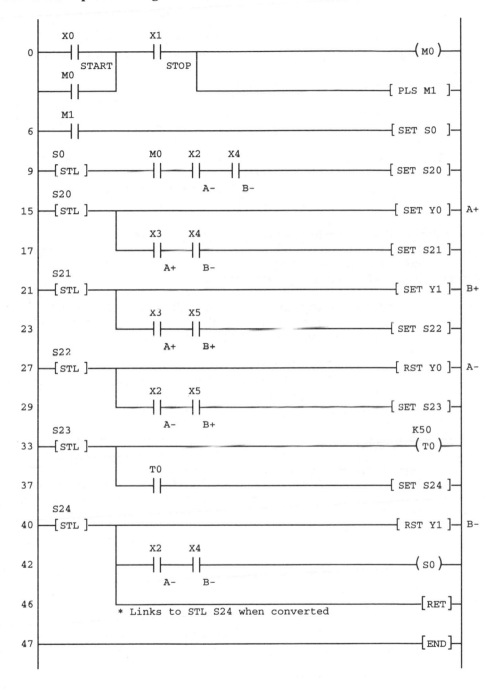

*Note

The RET instruction is entered directly without an input as shown on page 132, but on conversion, the RET instruction automatically connects to the STL S24 contact.

14.5 Principle of operation

1. Line 0
    (a) Inputs X0 and X1 are from the Start and Cycle stop buttons respectively.
    (b) Operating the Start input (X0) will energize the latch circuit of memory coil M0.
    (c) Also, memory coil M1 will be pulsed for one scan time.
2. Line 6
    (a) The momentary operation of M1 will set the state coil S0.
    (b) The use of the instruction Set enables an output coil to be turned ON and to remain ON, even when the input condition is no longer present.
    Hence even though the contacts of M1 are closed for one scan time the S0 coil will remain energized until it is Reset.
    (c) The S0 coil is used when initially starting and also to restart the next cycle (i.e. at line 42), when both pistons return to their initial state (i.e. A– and B–).
3. Line 9
The operation of all the following contacts will set the state coil S20:
    (a) The Step ladder contact STL S0.
    (b) The Start Cycle latch contact M0.
    (c) The A– contact X2 and the B– contact X4.
4. Line 15
    (a) The setting of the state coil S20 will cause the following to occur automatically:
        (i)   The STL contact S0 will open. This will have no effect on the state coil S20 as it has been set and hence will not be de-energized with the opening of STL S0.
        (ii) The STL S20 contact will close.
    (b) With the closure of STL S20 the output Y0 will then be energized and this will cause piston A to move to its A+ position.
    (c) When piston A reaches its A+ position, input X3 will close. This, plus the B– input X5, will set S21.
    (d) The setting of S21 will automatically cause STL 20 to open and STL S21 to close.
5. Line 21
    (a) The setting of the state coil S21 will cause the following to occur automatically.
        (i)   The STL contact S20 will open. This will have no effect on the output Y0 as it has been set and hence piston A will not be de-energized with the opening of STL S20.
        (ii) The STL S21 contact will close.
    (b) With the closure of STL S21 the output Y1 will be energized and this will cause piston B to move to its B+ position.
    (c) When piston B reaches its B+ position, input X5 will close. This, plus the A+ input X3, will set S22.
6. Line 27
    (a) The setting of the state coil S22 will cause the following to occur automatically:
        (i)   The STL contact S21 will open. This will have no effect on the output Y1 as it has been set, and hence piston B will not be de-energized with the opening of STL S21.
        (ii) The STL S22 contact will close.
    (b) With the closure of STL S22 the output Y0 will be reset and hence piston A will return to its A– position.
    (c) When piston A returns to its A– position, then input X2 will close. This, plus the B+ input X5, will set S23.

7. Line 33
   (a) The setting of the state coil S23, will automatically cause STL S22 to open and STL S23 to close.
   (b) With the closure of STL S23, the timer coil T0 will be energized.
   (c) When the timer T0 times out after 5 seconds, its T0 contact will close and this will set state coil S24.
8. Line 40
   (a) The operation of state coil S24 will automatically cause STL S23 to open and STL S24 to close.
   (b) The output Y1 is now Reset and this will cause piston B to return to its B– position.
   (c) With piston B returning to is B– position input X4 will close. This, plus the A– input X2, will energize the initial state coil S0.
   (d) As mentioned on page 129, when transferring to a distant state (i.e. a non-consecutive state), an Out instruction is used instead of a Set instruction.
9. Line 7
   With state S0 set, the contacts STL S0 will close and the cycle will recommence.
   If at any time during the automatic cycle, the Stop button is operated, then M0 will drop out. However, the process will continue until the end of the sequence, but with the reoperation of STL S0, it will not be possible to set state S20 because M0 is open. Thus the automatic cycle will stop.

14.6   Simulation – PNEU2

Using the switch box, simulate and monitor the operation of the step ladder project PNEU2.

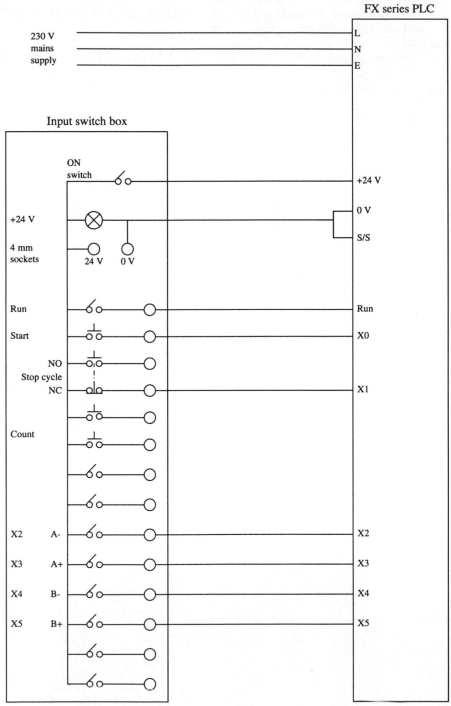

14.7 Monitoring – PNEU2

Using Decimal Device Monitoring, monitor the elements shown below and note how the S coils step from one state to the next.

Working	Area		Offline	FLASH1		FX	Ladder
Find	Save	Name	Copy	Move	Delete	Exchange	Test
Step	I/o	Text					

Monitor				Decimal				

——————————— Device Monitor ———————————

I/O	Name	Decimal	Pre/ASC	Hex	FEDC	BA98	7654	3210
X0		0		0				0
X1		1	☻	1				1
X2		1	☺	1				1
X3		0		0				0
X4		1	☺	1				1
X5		0		0				0
S0		0		0				0
S20		1	☺	1				1
S21		0		0				0
S22		0		0				0
S23		0		0				0
S24		0		0				0
Y0		1	☺	1				1
Y1		0		0				0
T0		0	K50	0	0000	0000	0000	0000

14.8 Wiring diagram – PNEU2

Connect the FX PLC to the pneumatic panel as shown on page 95. Press the Start button and note that the system will operate continuously until the Stop Cycle button is operated. However, the sequence will still continue until the end of the cycle.

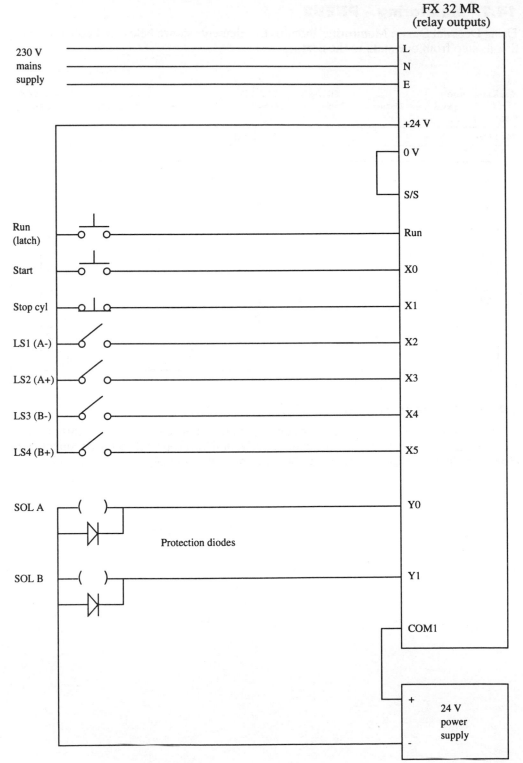

15
Multi-mode operation – PNEU3

Introduction

In many industrial PLC control systems it is necessary to have the following multi-mode operations:

1. Manual.
2. Return cycle (zero return).
3. Step cycle (jog).
4. Single cycle.
5. Automatic.

Using the instruction initial state (IST), these different operating conditions can be obtained automatically using selected X inputs, which are not shown on the ladder diagram.

With conventional ladder diagram programming, the change of operating condition can only be obtained via the PLC program.

15.1   The IST Instruction

The instruction ISTX10 S20 S24 indicates the following:

1. Inputs X10 to X17 are used as internal PLC control signals. Hence they are not shown on the ladder diagram.

Input	Function
X10	Manual operation
X11	Zero return
X12	Step cycle operation
X13	Single cycle operation
X14	Automatic operation
X16	Start auto/single cycle
X17	Stop auto/single cycle

   In an industrial application, inputs X10, X11, X12, X13 and X14 would be connected to a five-position rotary switch so that only one of these inputs could be ON at any one time. Inputs X16 and X17 would be connected to push buttons.
2. Step ladder contacts STL S20 to STL S24 are used for step cycle, single cycle and automatic cycle operation.
3. Further details concerning state memory coils are given on page 129.

Note

The instruction IST can only be used once in a program.

Ladder diagram – PNEU3

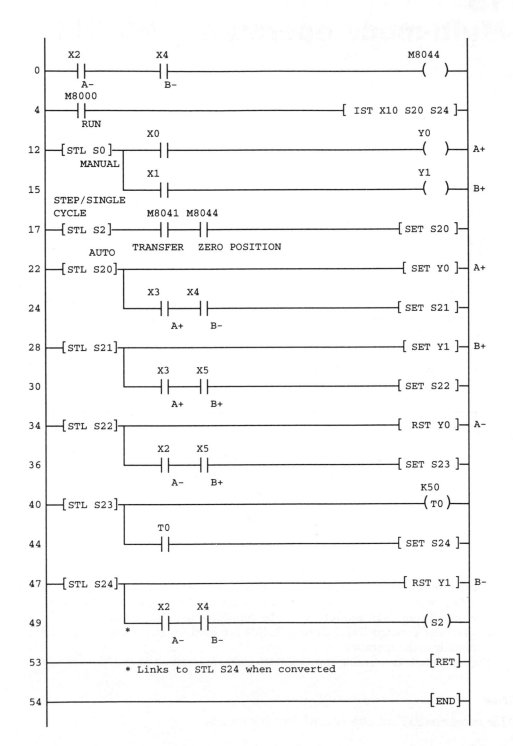

15.2 Simulation – PNEU3

Using the switch box, simulate and monitor the operation of the multi-sequence project PNEU3.

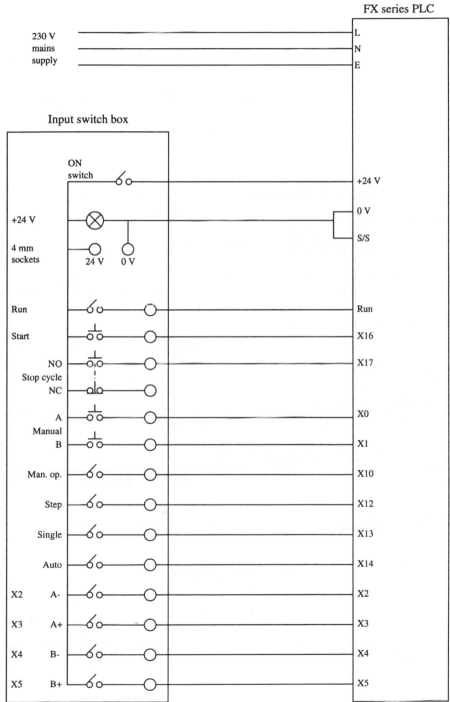

15.3 Manual operation

1. Initially ensure that all switches are OFF.
2. Switch ON the following:
   (a) RUN
   (b) X10   for manual operation.
3. Monitor the ladder diagram PNEU3.
4. Line 12
   With the closing of the input X10 (manual) switch, the step ladder contact STL S0 will automatically turn ON.
      Operating input X0 push button will turn output Y0 ON. This will energize piston A. Operating input X1 push button will turn output Y1 ON. This will energize piston B. Releasing the X0 and X1 push buttons will turn the respective outputs OFF.

15.4 Step cycle operation

In Step Cycle, the system goes through each separate operation of the machine cycle in turn, every time the Start button (X16) is pressed, until one complete cycle has been completed. This type of operation is also known as 'jog'.

1. Ensure that the manual input X10 is ON.
2. To simulate that both pistons are de-energized, operate inputs X2 (A–) and X4 (B–).
3. Turn input X10 OFF and X12 (Step Cycle) ON.
   Note the following:
   (a) Line 0
      With X2 and X4 both made, M8044 is ON. This is the zero-position condition.
   (b) Line 12
      STL S0 is OFF.
   (c) Line 17
      STL S2 is ON. This indicates Step/Single cycle operation.
4. Line 17
   Operate the Start push button, Input X16.
   Note the following:
   (a) While X16 is ON, the transfer start signal M8041 is also ON.
   (b) STL 2 is OFF; STL 20 is ON.
   (c) Output Y0 is ON. Piston A has been energized.
5. Set the limit switches for piston A being energized and piston B being de-energized (i.e. A+ and B–):

X2	OFF
X3	ON
X4	ON
X5	OFF

6. Repeatedly operating the Start push button, input X16 and setting the piston limit switches accordingly will cause the sequence to go through one complete machine cycle.

15.5 Single cycle operation

1. Ensure that one step cycle has been completed and that on line 17 the following can be observed:
   (a) STL S2 is ON.
   (b) M8041 is OFF.
2. Ensure that only the following limit switch inputs are operated:
   (a) X2 A–.
   (b) X4 B–.
   (c) With X2 and X4 operated and then M8044, the zero-position coil will also be ON.
3. Turn OFF the Step Cycle input X12.
4. Turn ON the Single Cycle input X13.
5. Press the Start push button X16 and note the following:
   (a) STL S2 is OFF.
   (b) STL S20 is ON.
   (c) Output Y0 is ON. Piston A has been energized.
6. Set the limit switches for Piston A being energized and Piston B being de-energized (i.e. A+ and B–):

X2	OFF
X3	ON
X4	ON
X5	OFF

7. Output Y1 will now come ON automatically, simulating the operation of piston B.
8. Setting the piston limit switches according to which outputs have operated will enable the sequence automatically to go through one complete machine cycle.
9. After completing one single cycle, further single cycles can be obtained by pressing the Start push button X16.

15.6 Automatic operation

1. Ensure that one single cycle has been completed and that on line 17 the following can be observed:
   (a) STL S2 is ON.
   (b) M8041 is OFF.
2. Ensure that only the following limit switch inputs are operated:
   (a) X2 A–.
   (b) X4 B–,
   (c) With X2 and X4 operated then M8044, the zero-position coil will also be ON.
3. Turn OFF the Single Cycle input X13.
4. Turn ON the Automatic Cycle input X14.
5. Operate the Start push button X16.
6. The system will now operate automatically, without stopping.
7. To stop the sequence, operate the Stop push button X17 and the system will complete the present cycle and then stop.
8. To repeat the automatic sequence, press the Start push button X16.

15.7 Pneumatic operation – PNEU3

Connect the FX PLC to the pneumatic panel as shown on page 95 and test the complete system for the four different cycles which can be used in multi-mode projects.

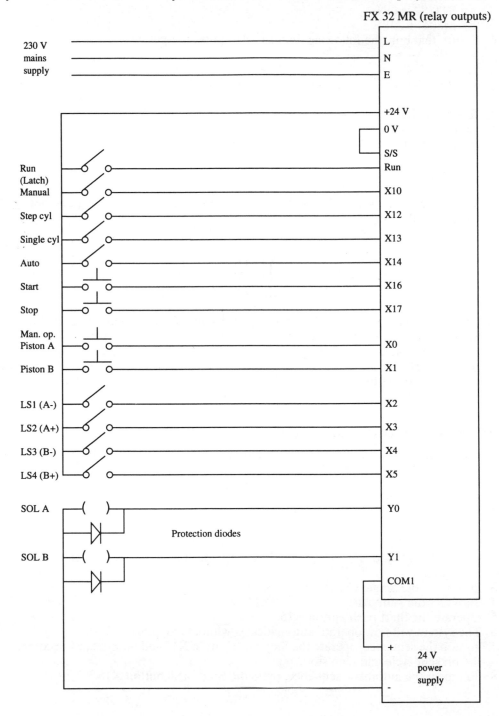

FX 32 MR (relay outputs)

16
Advanced PLC programming

The PLC programs produced so far basically replace conventional electromagnetic relay systems plus additional timers and counters, which are normally separate plug-in units. However, the programs which will now be produced are far more complex and enable the PLC to become more identified with computer-type operations.

16.1 Data registers

The starting point for these advanced programs, is the data register.

The data register is basically a collection of 16 auxiliary memory coils which are linked together to store in numerical values in binary form. In addition it is possible to link two data registers together (i.e. the equivalent of 32 M coils) to enable even larger numbers to be stored.

Register size	Number range
1 (16 bits)	0–65 535
2 (32 bits)	0–4295 million

Format – 16 bit data register

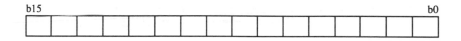

b0   least significant bit
b15   most significant bit

Each bit of the data register stores either a logic 0 or a logic 1.

16.2 Number representation using binary

In the binary system only the values 0 and 1 can be used, but by using a number of binary bits it is possible for them to be equal to any standard denary (decimal) number.

Decimal value	Binary value
0	0000 0000 0000 0000
1	0000 0000 0000 0001
2	0000 0000 0000 0010
3	0000 0000 0000 0011
4	0000 0000 0000 0100
5	0000 0000 0000 0101
6	0000 0000 0000 0110
7	0000 0000 0000 0111
8	0000 0000 0000 1000
9	0000 0000 0000 1001
10	0000 0000 0000 1010
.	.
.	.
.	.
255	0000 0000 1111 1111
256	0000 0001 0000 0000
257	0000 0001 0000 0001
.	.
.	.
4095	0000 1111 1111 1111
4096	0001 0000 0000 0000
4097	0001 0000 0000 0001
.	.
.	.
65 535	1111 1111 1111 1111

16.3 Converting a binary number to its denary equivalent

It is possible to convert a binary number to its denary equivalent by assigning a denary weighting value to each of the binary columns. For ease of understanding, only 8 bit numbers will be considered.

The denary weighting values are as follows:

Column number	Weighting value
1	1
2	2
3	4
4	8
5	16
6	32
7	64
8	128

Example

Convert the binary number 1001 1101 to its denary equivalent.

Note

msb is the most significant bit: lsb is the least significant bit

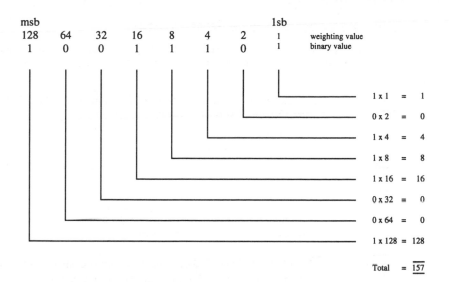

Hence 1001 1101 = 157.

16.4 Binary numbers and binary-coded decimal

A binary value can be displayed in two different ways:

1. Pure binary.
2. Binary coded decimal (BCD).

Pure binary

Consider the following binary number:

$$0010\ 0101\ 1001\ 0110$$

In pure binary this is equal to 9622.

Binary-coded decimal

In BCD the binary numbers are grouped into blocks of four binary digit. Each block of binary digits is then converted to its denary equivalent.

$$
\begin{array}{cccc}
1001 & 0110 & 0010 & 0010 \\
| & | & | & | \\
9 & 6 & 2 & 2
\end{array}
$$

The BCD binary pattern is now 1001 0110 0010 0010 for it to equal 9622.

The reason for using BCD is that each block of four digits can be output to a binary-to-decimal decoder chip, whose outputs can then be connected to a four-digit 0-9999 display.

16.5 Advanced programming instructions

The following advanced instructions will be used for the applications, which are now to be developed (a full list of the advanced instructions are in the Mitsubushi FX programming manual):

1. addp d0 k2 d0   Add 2 to the existing contents of D0 and store the result back into D0, each time the input condition goes positive.

```
    X0
├───┤ ├──────────────────────────────────────────[ ADDP  D0  K2  D0 ]──┤
```

The instruction will not be executed again until the input i.e. X0 is opened and then reclosed.

2. addp d0 k5 d1   Add 5 to the existing contents of D0 and store the result in D1, each time the input condition goes positive.

3. bcd d0 k4y0   Transfer 16 bits of data from D0 to Y0–Y17, in BCD format (i.e. from 0 to 9999), each time the instruction is executed.

```
    X0
├───┤ ├──────────────────────────────────────────[ BCD  D0  K4Y0 ]──┤
```

While the input (i.e. X0) is closed, the instruction will be executed during each scan of the program, that is every few milliseconds. The k value indicates the number of bits to be transferred:

k1   4 bits
k2   8 bits
k3   12 bits
k4   16 bits

4. bin k2x0 d0   Load data register D0 with 2×4 bits of data from X0–X7 in BCD format.

bin = BCD INPUT

Input number range 0–99.

5. cmp d0 k10 m1   Each time this instruction is executed, the logic states of the internal memory coils M1, M2 and M3 will indicate the result of the comparison:
M1 ON if D0 > 10
M2 ON if D0 = 10
M3 ON if D0 < 10

6. decp d0   Decrement the contents of D0, each time the input condition goes positive.

7. divp d16 k100 d18   Divide the existing contents of d16 by 100 and store the result in D18 and D19, each time the input condition goes positive.

$$\left.\begin{array}{l} \text{D18 (quotient)} \\ \text{D19 (remainder)} \end{array}\right\} = \dfrac{\text{D16}}{100}$$

Quotient part of the result stored in D18; remainder part of the result stored in D19.

8. fmov k0 d0 k4   Clear four data registers from D0 to D3 inclusive.

9. incp d0   Increment the contents of data register D0, each time the input condition goes positive.

10. mov d0 k4y0   Transfer 16 bits of data from D0 to Y0–Y17, in binary format (i.e. from 0 to 65 535).

11. mov k0 d0   Move (i.e. load) the value 0 into data register D0.

12. mov k104 d0   Load the value 104 into data register D0.

13. movp k0 d0   Clear data register D0, each time the input condition goes positive.

14. mov k2x0 d0   Load data register D0 with 2 × 4 bits of data from X0 to X7. Input number range 0–255.

15. mulp d2 k10 d3   Multiply the existing contents of d2 by 10, each time the input

$$\left.\begin{array}{l} \text{D3 (lower 16 bits)} \\ \text{D4 (upper 16 bits)} \end{array}\right\} = 10 \times \text{D2}.$$

condition goes positive. Lower 16 bits of the result are stored in d3; upper 16 bits of the result are stored in d4.

16. rst d0   Clear the contents of data register D0. Identical to mov k0 d0

17. subp d0 K5 d1   Subtract 5 from the existing contents of D0 and store the result in D1, each time the input condition goes positive.

$$\text{D1} = \text{D0} - 5$$

18.   D0
   –(T0)–   Load timer T0 with the contents of data register D0. This is used to change the value of the time delay whilst the program is being executed.

17
Application programs using advanced instructions

The following application programs will now be developed in this chapter which will enable skills to be acquired, in the use of some of the Mitsubishi advanced PLC instructions.

1. COUNT4   Binary counter, display of an accumulating count in binary.
2. COUNT5   Modify COUNT4, to display the accumulating count in BCD.
3. COUNT6   Counter program in which the input pulses are counted during an unsynchronized 5 second period and which displays the output in BCD at the end of the 5 seconds.
4. COUNT7   Modify COUNT6 to ensure that the first input pulse, starts the five second timing period.
5. COUNT8   Counter program having upper and lower limits:
   • Turn Y0 ON   if the number of input pulses is equal to or greater than 10 at the end of the 5 second timing period.
   • Turn Y0 OFF   if the number of input pulses is less than 10, at the end of the 5 second timing period.
6. DELAY1   Display the elapsed time in seconds and tenths of seconds, between the operation of inputs X0 and X1.
7. DELAY2   Display the elapsed time between the operation of inputs X0 and X1. In addition:
   • If the elapsed time is in the range 15 to 20 seconds, turn Y0 ON.
   • Else if outside this range turn Y1 ON.
8. DELAY3   Modify a required time delay in the range 15 to 20 seconds by incrementing or decrementing inputs X0 or X1 respectively, whilst the program is being executed. The required time delay is displayed on outputs Y10 to Y17.
9. DELAY4   Modify ON/OFF time delays in the range 0.5 to 9.9 seconds by changing the X0–X7 input value, whilst the program is being executed.

17.1   Binary counter – COUNT4

A simple counting system will now be produced in which a push button will simulate pulses coming from a transducer. In an industrial application, the transducer could be monitoring the rotation of a toothed gear wheel connected to, for example, a conveyor system. The total number of pulses is displayed on the output LEDs in pure binary form.

System – block diagram

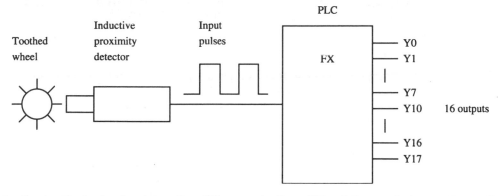

As the toothed wheel rotates, the difference in the width of the gap between the teeth and the inductive proximity detector will change.

Within the detector is a small magnet and coil, and as the air gap between the gear wheel and the detector changes, it will cause a change in the magnetic field within the detector, which, in turn, will induce voltage pulses into the coil. These pulses are now fed into the PLC, where they can be:

1. Counted.
2. Displayed as an incrementing value on the Y outputs, Y0–Y17.

Ladder diagram – COUNT4

This counter circuit will be used, to count the incoming pulses and display the incrementing count in pure binary form.

Principle of operation

1. Line 0
   The closing of input contact X0 will cause the data register D0 to be cleared, by loading it with 0. The use of 'P' ensures that this operation only occurs when the input X0 is operated and not each time the program is scanned.
2. Line 6
   The input pulses are simulated by the opening and closing of input X1. Each time input X1 is closed the contents of data register D0 are incremented by one.

3. Line 10

   With Input X0 closed, the contents of D0 are transferred to the 16 outputs Y0 to Y17. X0 remains closed, until it is required for resetting D0 (line 0).

Entering the program

Most advanced instructions can be entered simply by typing them in from the keyboard. Hence, the program COUNT4 can be entered as shown below.

Instruction		Keyboard Entry	
1. X0	1	x0	<ent>
2. MOVP K0 D0		movp	<ent>
		k0	<ent>
		d0	<ent>
3. X1	1	x1	<ent>
4. INCP D0		incp	<ent>
		d0	<ent>
5. X0	1	x0	<ent>
6. MOV D0 K4Y0		mov	<ent>
		d0	<ent>
		k4y0	<ent>
7. END		end	<ent>

Alternative method

An alternative, but longer, method is shown below.

Keypress	Operation
8	Select first set of ladder diagram instructions.
F9	Toggle between first and second set of instructions. Select required instruction.
F10	Display and select third set of instructions.

Program display – COUNT4

After the program has been converted, the ladder diagram display will be as shown below.

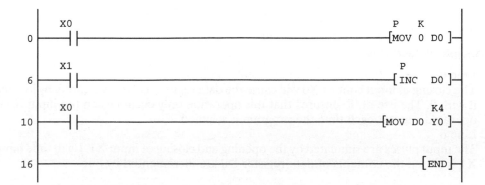

Testing the program

Download the program to the FX PLC and test the program using the following:

1. An ON/OFF switch for the input   X0
2. A push-button for the input   X1

Program Monitoring

To monitor the operation of the program in real time, carry out the following operations:

1. Display the ladder diagram.
2. Press <F2>.
3. Press <F8>.
4. Wait until the word 'Monitor' flashes ON and OFF.
5. Press <F5> to enter monitor edit mode. This will enable the names of those program elements to be entered, whose contents are required to be monitored whilst the program is being executed.
6. The display now becomes as shown below.

```
Working area              Offline   COUNT4            FX          Ladder
Find      Save    Name    Copy      Move    Delete    Exchange    Test
Step      I/o     Text
```

```
Monitor Edit Mode
```

7. Enter the following:
   X0 <ent>.
   X1 <ent>.
   D0 <ent>.
      This will enable the contents of data register D0 to be monitored whilst the program is being executed.

8. Press <esc> to return to monitor mode.
9. The display now becomes as shown below.

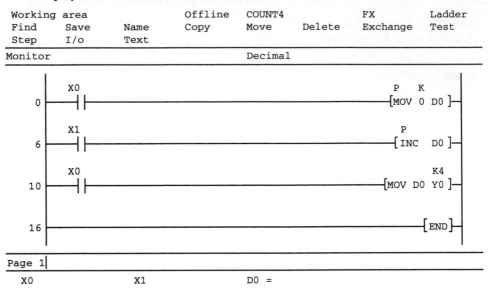

Decimal device monitor

The decimal device monitor enables selected device elements to be monitored without the use of a ladder diagram. The advantage of this type of monitor is that more than eight elements can be simultaneously monitored.

To use the decimal device monitor, carry out the following from Ladder Monitor Mode.

1. Press   <esc>
        <F9>
        <F8>
2. Since the elements X0, X1 and D0 were previously entered whilst in ladder edit mode, these same elements do not have to be re-entered for Decimal Device Monitoring.
3. Each time the input push button X1 is operated, the contents of data register D0 will be displayed in:
   (a) Decimal
   (b) ASCII
   (c) Hexadecimal
   (d) Binary
4. After the X1 push button has been operated 10 times, the display will become as shown below.

Working Area			Offline	COUNT4		FX	Ladder
Find	Save	Name	Copy	Move	Delete	Exchange	Test
Step	I/o	Text					

Monitor   Decimal

					Device Monitor			
I/O	Name	Decimal	Pre/ASC	Hex	FEDC	BA98	7654	3210
X0		1	☺	1				1
X1		0		0				0
D0		10		A	0000	0000	0000	1010

17.2 COUNT5 – BCD output

Each time the input X1 is operated, the output LEDs will display an incrementing count in BCD format. That is, the output number can only be in the range 0–9999.

Note

The ladder diagram instructions will now be shown as they are entered from the keyboard and not how they actually appear on the displayed ladder diagram. Hence from now on,

```
        P   K
    –[MOV 0 D0]–
```
will be shown as –[MOVP K0 D0]–

The space between each part of the instruction is where the <ent> key is to be pressed.

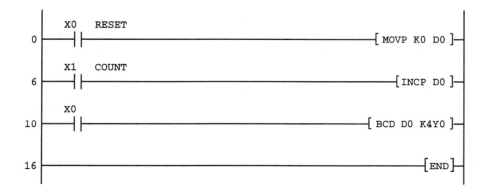

Principle of operation – COUNT5

1. Line 0
   Each time input X0 is operated, data register D0 is cleared to zero.
2. Line 6
   Each time input X1 is operated, the contents of the data register will be incremented (i.e. increased) by one.
3. Line 10
   While input X0 remains operated, the 16 bit contents of D0 are transferred (i.e. copied) in BCD form to the 16 Y outputs, Y0–Y17. Hence displayed on the Y outputs will be an incrementing count in BCD form from 0 to 9999.

Monitoring

Using decimal device monitoring, monitor the following elements:

1. X0
2. X1
3. D0

17.3 COUNT6

Produce a PLC ladder diagram, which will count the number of pulses input during any unsynchronized 5 second period. The count is to be displayed in BCD format on the output LEDs. The term unsynchronized, means there is no direct connection between the timing signals and the count pulses.

Timer T0

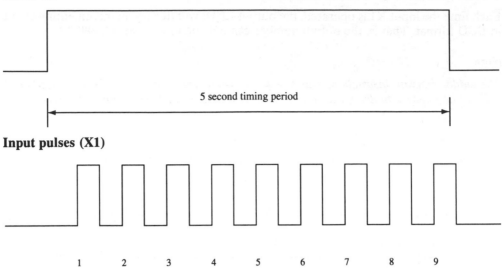

5 second timing period

Input pulses (X1)

1 2 3 4 5 6 7 8 9

From the above timing waveforms, it can be seen that if eight pulses are input during the 5 second timing period, then this value will be displayed on the Y outputs Y0–Y17.

Solution – COUNT6

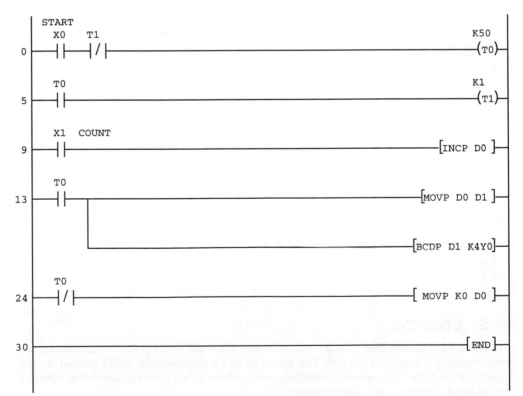

Principle of operation – COUNT6

1. Lines 0 and 5
   Lines 0 and 5 produce an ON/OFF waveform, whilst input X0 remains ON.
2. Consider the timer T0 waveform shown below.

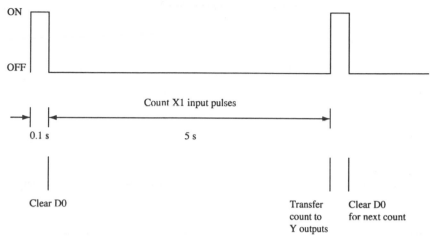

The ON time is determined by the time allocated to timer T1; the OFF time is determined by the time allocated to timer T0.

3. Line 9
   Each time input X1 is operated, data register D0 is incremented.
4. Line 13
   On the rising edge of T0, that is after the 5 second delay has elapsed, the contents of D0 are transferred in binary format to data register D1 and displayed in BCD format on the output LEDs Y0–Y17.
5. Line 24
   On the falling edge of T0, that is when its normally closed contacts make, data register D0 is cleared to zero.

Monitoring – COUNT6

Using decimal device monitoring, monitor the following:

Working Area			Offline	COUNT4		FX	Ladder
Find	Save	Name	Copy	Move	Delete	Exchange	Test
Step	I/o	Text					

Monitor				Decimal			

—————————— Device Monitor ——————————							
I/O	Name	Decimal	Prc/ASC	Hex	FEDC	BA98	7654	3210
X0		0		0				0
X1		0		0				0
T0		0	K50	0	0000	0000	0000	0000
T1		0	K1	0	0000	0000	0000	0000
D0		0		0	0000	0000	0000	0000
D1		10		A	0000	0000	0000	1010
K4Y0		16		10	0000	0000	0001	0000

The display shown above, is obtained after there have been a total of 10 input pulses during the 5 second timing period.

Note

When monitoring the output K4Y0 i.e. Y0–Y17, the binary pattern corresponds to the output LEDs in BCD. However, the decimal value (i.e. 16) is not the true value of the number of input pulses. It is the equivalent decimal number of the output binary pattern, in true binary. Thus care must be taken when monitoring outputs directly.

17.4 COUNT7

Modify COUNT6 so that the first count pulse, which is now from input X0 via the push button, will start the 5 second delay period. This enables a true measurement to be carried out of the number of input pulses which have occurred within the 5 second delay period.

Solution – COUNT7

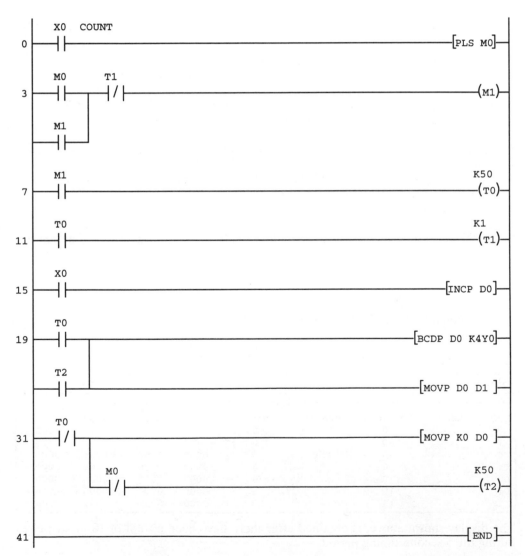

Waveforms – COUNT7

Input X0

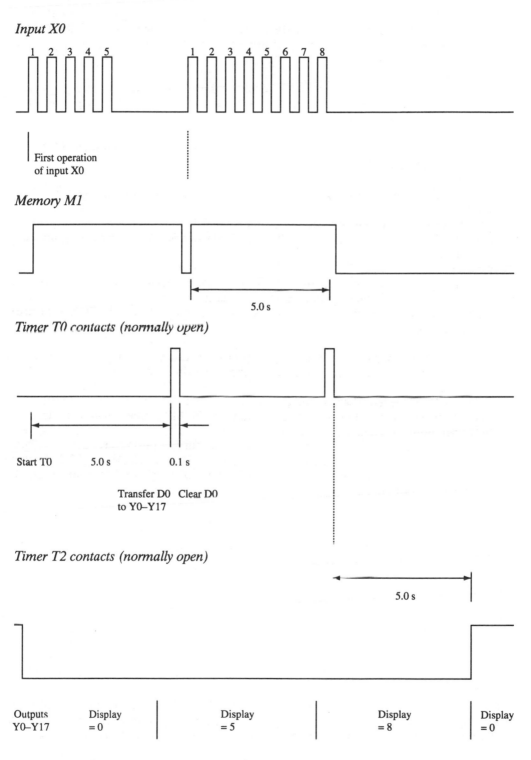

First operation
of input X0

Memory M1

5.0 s

Timer T0 contacts (normally open)

Start T0   5.0 s   0.1 s

Transfer D0   Clear D0
to Y0–Y17

Timer T2 contacts (normally open)

5.0 s

| Outputs Y0–Y17 | Display = 0 | Display = 5 | Display = 8 | Display = 0 |

Principle of operation – COUNT7

1. Lines 0–3
   The first time the count input X0 is operated, the internal memory coil M0 is pulsed for one scan time. The momentary closure of the M0 contacts will latch ON the internal memory M1.
2. Lines 7–11
   The closing of M1 will start the 5 second timer T0. Hence the timer is now synchronized to the first input pulse of X0. Timers T0 and T1 will now produce the T0 waveform shown on page 159.
3. Line 15
   During the 5 second time delay of timer T0, each time the input X0 is turned ON and OFF, the contents of D0 are incremented by one.
4. Line 19
   At the end of the 5 second delay, the T0 contacts will close and the contents of D0 will be:
   (a) Displayed in BCD format on the outputs Y0–Y17.
   (b) Transferred to data register D1. This data register is used solely for monitoring purposes.
5. Line 11
   At the end of the 0.1 second time delay of timer T1, its normally closed contact at line 3 will open, causing the M1 latch circuit to drop out. Hence the coil of timer T0 will de-energize, followed almost immediately by the coil of timer T1 also de-energizing.
6. Line 31
   With the normally closed contact of T0 remaking, this will cause the contents of data register D0 to be cleared to zero. At the same time, the 5 second Timer T2 is energized.
   Timer T2 is energized when the T0 contacts reclose. However, should another set of count pulses occur while T2 is timing out, then the M0 contacts will open and the timer will immediately be de-energized.
   The function of T2 is to clear the display when no further pulses have been received during the 5 second period from the remaking of the T0 contacts. When T2 does time out its contacts at line 19 will close, which will transfer the cleared contents of D0 to the Y0 - Y17 outputs.

Monitoring

Using Decimal Device Monitoring, monitor the following:

1. X0
2. T0
3. T2
4. D0
5. D1
6. K4Y0

17.5   COUNT8

Modify COUNT7 so that the output Y0 will turn ON if the number of input pulses is equal to or greater than 10, during a 5 second time period. In addition, display the input pulse count after the 5 second delay period on the Y10–Y17 output LEDs.

Solution – COUNT8

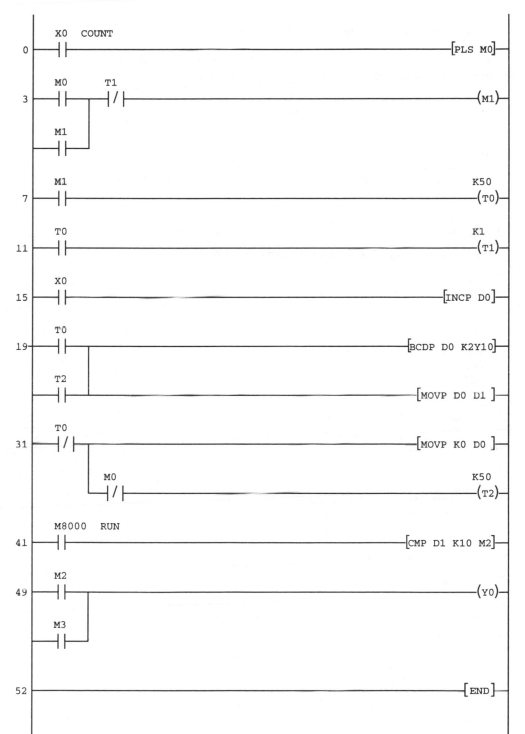

Principle of operation – COUNT8

1. Lines 0–31
   COUNT8 up to and including line 31 is identical to COUNT7.
2. Line 41
   The contents of D1 are now compared with the value 10 and, depending on the result of the comparison, the following M coils are affected:

   M2 ON if D1 > 10 D1 greater than 10
   M3 ON if D1 = 10 D1 equal to 10
   M4 ON if D1 < 10 D1 less than 10

3. Line 49
   If the contents of D1 are equal to or greater than 10, then M2 and/or M3 are energized and hence output Y0 is turned ON. Else, if the contents of D0 are less than 10, then M4 is energized and hence output Y0 is turned OFF.

Monitoring

Using Decimal Device Monitoring, monitor the following:

1. X0
2. T0
3. T2
4. D0
5. D1
6. K2Y10
7. M2
8. M3
9. M4
10. Y0

Note

If:

1. *The number of pulses > 10, M2 ON.*
2. *The number of pulses = 10, M3 ON.*
3. *The number of pulses < 10, M4 ON.*

17.6 DELAY1

The program shown on the facing page measures the time delay between the operation of two input switches X0 and X1 and outputs the result in BCD format, in seconds and tenths of seconds.

Solution – DELAY1

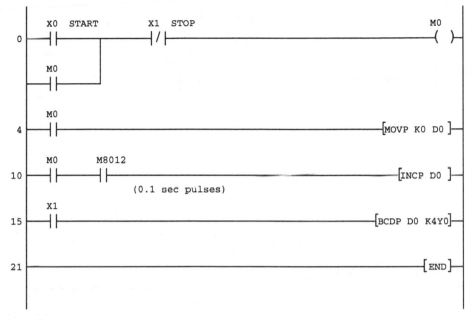

Note

Refer to page 128, for further details on the special M coil M8012.

Principle of operation – DELAY1

1. Line 0
   When X0 is operated M0 will also operate and latch via its own contact.
2. Line 4
   When internal contact M0 closes, its positive rising edge will cause data register D0 to be cleared.
3. Line 10
   Every 0.1 seconds, when the M8012 contact closes, the contents of data register D0 are incremented by one.
4. Lines 0 and 15
   When contact X1 is operated, this will cause the following to happen:
   (a) The M0 latch circuit will be broken.
   (b) The contents of data register D0 will be output to the 16 outputs, Y0–Y17.
5. Hence the output LEDs are displaying the time delay between the operation of inputs X0 and X1.

Monitoring

Using Decimal Device Monitoring, monitor the following.

1. X0
2. X1
3. D0
4. K4Y0

17.7 DELAY2

Modify DELAY1 to include the following changes:

1. If the time delay between input X1 operating and input X2 operating is between 15 and 20 seconds, then Turn Y0 ON. Else, if the time delay is outside these values then, turn Y1 ON.
2. Display the time delay from 0 to 99.9 seconds on the 12 outputs, Y4–Y17

Solution – DELAY2

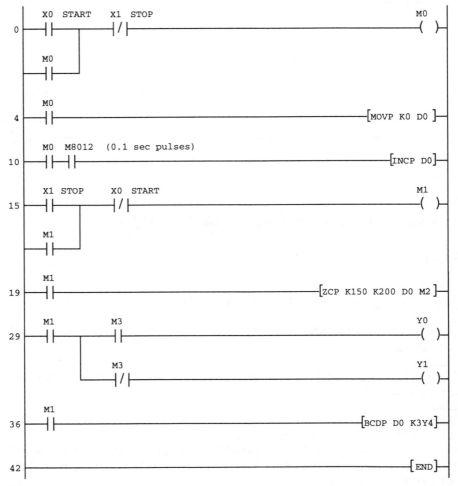

Principle of operation – DELAY2

1. Line 0
   When X0 is operated M0 will also operate and latch via its own contact.
2. Line 4
   When internal contact M0 closes, its positive rising edge will cause data register D0, to be cleared.
3. Line 10
   Every 0.1 seconds, when the M8012 contact closes, the contents of data register D0

are incremented by one. Hence for a 15 to 20 second time delay, the contents of D0 will be between 150 and 200.

4. Line 15

At the end of the timing period, when contact X1 operates, the following will occur:

(a) The internal memory coil M1 will be energized, which will then latch over its own contact.

(b) Line 0

X1 opens, which causes the M0 latch circuit to become de-energized.

5. Line 19

The instruction Zone Compare is a comparison between a lower limit (i.e. 150) and an upper limit (i.e. 200), with the contents of data register D0. Memory coils M2, M3 and M4 indicate the result of the comparison:

M2 ON, if D0 is less than K150.

M3 ON, if D0 is greater than or equal to K150, or D0 is less than or equal to K200.

M4 ON, if D0 is greater than K200.

Hence, if the time delay between operating the start button X0 and the stop button X1 is between 15 and 20 seconds, then M3 will operate. However, if the time delay is outside these limits then M3 will not operate.

6. Line 29

At the instant the stop button is operated, M1 is energized.

If the time delay is between 15 and 20 seconds, the contents of D0 will be between 150 and 200, M3 will operate and output Y0 will become energized. However, if the time delay is outside this range, then M3 will not operate and hence Y1 will be energized via the normally closed contact of M3.

7. Line 36

The contents of D0 are now transferred to the Y outputs Y4–Y17, using the instruction BCDP D0 K3Y4.

Monitoring

Using Decimal Device Monitoring, monitor the following:

1. X0
2. X1
3. M0
4. M1
5. D0
6. M2
7. M3
8. M4
9. Y0
10. Y1
11. K4Y0

17.8 DELAY3

This program will enable the value of a time delay to be varied, whilst the program is being executed.

1. The required time delay is in the range 10 to 20 seconds and the time is varied by operating inputs X1 and X2.

(a) Operating pushbutton X0 starts the time delay.

(b) Operating pushbutton X1 increments the required delay in 1 second steps, to a maximum of 20 seconds.

(c) Operating pushbutton X2 decrements the required delay in 1 second steps, to a minimum of 10 seconds.

2. The required delay is to be displayed on the Y10–Y17 outputs.
3. At the end of the time delay period, the Y0 output is energized.
4. This is part of an industrial control program, which enables an operator to change process times, but within set limits.

Solution – DELAY3

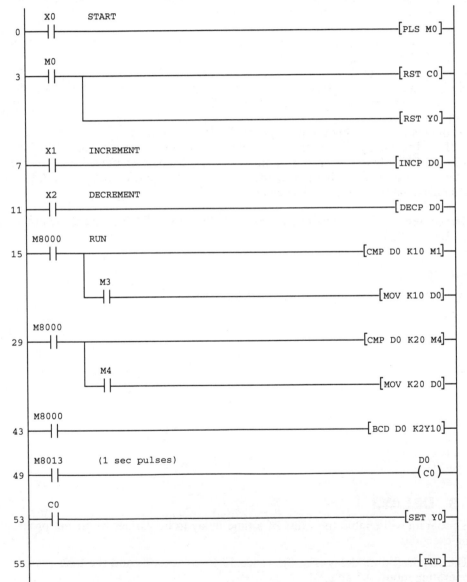

Principle of operation – DELAY3

1. Line 0
   The operation of input X0 pulses for one scan time, M0.
2. Line 3
   The momentary operation of M0 enables both the counter C0 and the output Y0 to be reset.
3. Line 7
   The operation of the input push button X1 will increment the contents of data register D0.
4. Line 11
   The operation of input X2 decrements the contents of data register D0.
5. Line 15
   The instruction compare is used to compare the contents of D0 with the lower limit of 10. If the contents of D0 have been decremented below 10, then the operation of M3 will restore the contents of D0 back to 10.
6. Line 29
   The instruction compare is used to compare the contents of D0 with the upper limit of 20. If the contents of D0 have been incremented above 20, then the operation of M4 will restore the contents of D0 back to 20.
7. Line 43
   Using the instruction ─[BCD D0 K2Y10]─, the contents of D0 are displayed on the outputs Y10 – Y17 in BCD format
8. Line 49
   The instruction

   ```
        D0
   ─(C0)─
   ```

   enables the Counter C0 to be incremented up to the value stored in D0.
   The counter is incremented using 1 second pulses from M8013. Hence, whatever value is stored in D0 will be the time taken in seconds for counter C0 to operate.
9. Line 53
   The operation of the C0 contacts after the required time delay will cause output Y0 to become energized.

Note

From the above description it can be seen that the time delay is started by the operation of input X0 and at the end of the delay, output Y0 comes ON. The time delay can be varied by the operation of the inputs X1 and X2, within the range 10 to 20 seconds.

Monitoring

Using Decimal Device Monitoring, monitor the following.
1. D0
2. M3
3. M4
4. C0
5. Y0

17.9 DELAY4

Produce a PLC program which will enter a value from 0 to 99 in BCD format, from inputs X0–X7. This value will be used to modify the time delay of timers T0 and T1, from 0.5 to 9.9 seconds, whilst the program is being executed. The output from T0 will be used to turn output Y0 ON and OFF at a rate determined by the inputs X0–X7.

Solution – DELAY4

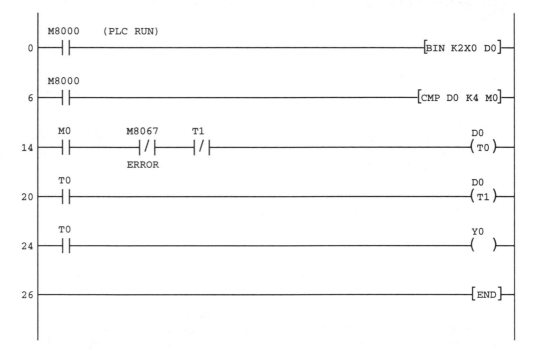

Principle of operation – DELAY4

1. Line 0
   Contact M8000 is an internal memory contact which effectively closes when the PLC is switched to RUN. The input value of X0–X7 is now loaded into data register D0 in BCD format (i.e. 0–99). If a units' value greater than nine or a tens' value greater than 90 is entered, then the system will not function correctly
2. Line 6
   The input value from X0 to X7 is now compared with the value 4:
   M0 ON, if D0 > 4.
   M1 ON, if D0 = 4.
   M2 ON, if D0 < 4.
   This is done to ensure that, should a time value of less than 0.5 seconds be entered, the system will not operate and the output relay connected to Y0 will not be switched ON and OFF at too fast a rate.
3. Line 14
   M0 will be closed if the required time delay is at least 0.5 seconds.
   M8067 is an error signal used with the instruction BIN, to indicate that the units' input value has exceeded the value of nine and/or the tens' value, has exceeded 90. If

M8067 is operated, it can only be cleared by ensuring that the input value is in the correct range and then switching the PLC to stop.

Assuming that the input time delay is at least 0.5 seconds and M8067 has not been operated, then at the start of the program, contact T1 will be closed. The timer coil T0 is loaded with the contents of data register D0, which is the BCD value input from X0–X7.

4. Line 20

When timer T0 times out, then timer T1 is also loaded with the input from X0–X7. Hence timers T0 and T1 are connected as an ON/OFF circuit, whose flash rate is determined by the inputs X0–X7.

5. Line 24

With T0 turning ON/OFF, Y0 will also turn ON/OFF.

Monitoring

Using Decimal Device Monitoring, monitor the following:

1. K2X0
2. D0
3. M0
4. M8067
5. T0
6. T1
7. Y0

18
Sub-system programs

The programs which will be developed in this chapter will enable an understanding to be obtained of the sub-system type of programs which are available within the Mitsubishi FX PLC. The sub-system programs which will be covered in this chapter are as follows:

1. Shift registers.
2. Master control.
3. Index registers.
4. Sub-routines.
5. Interrupts.

18.1 Shift registers

A shift register is a combination of memory elements, which are linked together to store data and then shift the stored data in a leftwards or rightwards direction.

Shift register applications

The following is a list of applications which require the use of a shift register.

1. Parallel-to-serial conversion.
2. Serial-to-parallel conversion.
3. Simple multiplication and division by 2, 4, 8, 16, etc.
4. Storage and shifting of data relating to industrial processes.
5. Scanning of input signals sequentially, that is multiplexing.

Shift register – SHIFT1

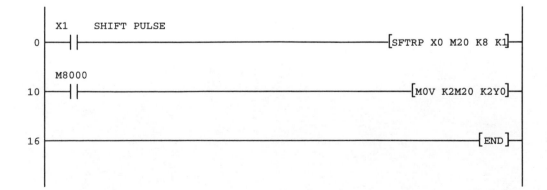

Shift register operation

The basic principle of operation is that the memory coils M27–M20 are combined to become 1 × 8 bit shift register. The input data is determined by the logic state of input X0.

The shift right signal is obtained from the input X1. That is, whenever X1 is operated, the contents of the shift register are shifted one place right, after which the logic state of X0 is copied into the msb (M27) of the shift register.

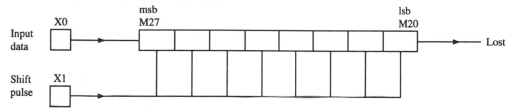

Principle of operation – SHIFT1

1. Line 0
   Each time input X1 is operated, the following occurs:
   (a) The contents of the shift register M27–M20 are shifted one position right.
   (b) The contents of X0 are loaded into the most significant bit (msb) of the shift register (i.e. M27).
2. Line 10
   The contents of the shift register are monitored on the outputs Y7–Y0.

Note

When a logic 1 in the lsb (i.e. M20) is shifted out of the register, its value becomes lost. However, when using rotate instructions, the output is saved in M8022.

Monitoring

Using Decimal Device Monitoring, monitor the following elements:

1. X0
2. X1
3. K2M20

Set the data input (X0) for each condition as shown in the table below, and then operate the shift button (X1).

Input data (X0)	M27 (Y7)	M26 (Y6)	M25 (Y5)	M24 (Y4)	M23 (Y3)	M22 (Y2)	M21 (Y1)	M20 (Y0)
				Shift register outputs				
0	0	0	0	0	0	0	0	0
1	1	0	0	0	0	0	0	0
0	0	1	0	0	0	0	0	0
0	0	0	1	0	0	0	0	0
1	1	0	0	1	0	0	0	0
0	0	1	0	0	1	0	0	0
1	1	0	1	0	0	1	0	0
1	1	1	0	1	0	0	1	0
0	0	1	1	0	1	0	0	1

18.2 Master Control

The Master Control (MC) instruction enables a group of instructions to be controlled by a single master contact, which effectively switches power to those instructions.

The MCR instruction is used at the end of the group of instructions and any instructions following the MCR instruction are not under the control of the master contact.

Nesting level

The nesting level number refers to the number of an MC circuit which is linked within other MC circuits.

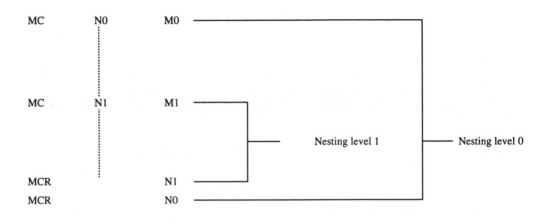

Ladder diagram – MC1

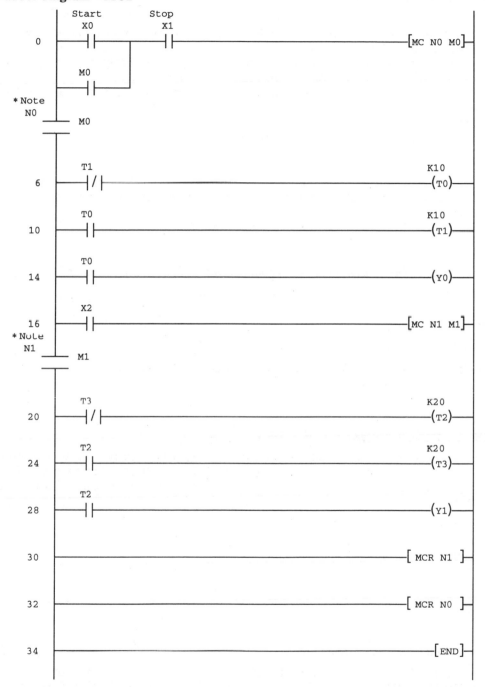

Note

The master contacts shown on the ladder diagram above cannot be entered from the keyboard. They appear on the diagram, after it has been converted to an instruction program.

Principle of operation

1. Line 0
   Operation of the start push button will operate the instruction $-$[MC NO MO]$-$, which will cause the following to occur:
   (a) Memory coil M0 will be energized and latch over its own contact.
   (b) The operation of M0 will now energize the master contact M0.
   This effectively enables all of the nesting level 0 instructions from line 6 to line 16 to become operative.
2. Lines 6–14
   The two timers T0 and T1 are interconnected to form a 1 second ON, 1 second OFF circuit.
3. Line 16
   Operation of Input X2, now energizes the nesting level 1 instructions, which are controlled by master contact M1. This now energizes a 2 second ON/OFF circuit.

Note

For the nesting level 1 instructions to become operative, both master contacts M0 and M1 have to be ON.

Monitoring – MC1

Using the ladder diagram, monitor the operation of MC1:

1. When first of all input X0 is operated, followed by input X2.
2. Only input X2 is operated.

18.3   Index registers V and Z

Index registers are similar to data registers in that they can store 16 bit data. However, the main function of these registers is to provide an offset value to other PLC elements. The FX PLC elements (which can be used with index registers are listed below):

1. Inputs   X
2. Outputs   Y
3. Memory coils M
4. State coils   S
5. Timers   T
6. Counters   C
7. Registers   D

Typical index register instructions

1. MOV K5 Z   Load the Z register with the constant value of 5.
2. MOV D20Z D1   With Z = 5, move the contents of D(20 + 5) (i.e. D25) into data register D1.
3. INCP V   Increment on a closing input the contents of index register V.

4. DIVP V D0 D1   Divide the contents of index register V by the contents of D0 and store the results as follows:

For example

$$\frac{11}{4}$$

D1 contains the quotient = 2.
D2 contains the remainder = 3.

5. MOVP D2 Z   Move on a closing input the contents of D2 into index register Z.

6. BCD D20Z K4Y0   If Z = 0, output the contents of D20 to Y0–Y17 in BCD.

If Z = 1, output the contents of D21 to Y0–Y17 in BCD.

.
.

.
If Z = 5, output the contents of D25 to Y0–Y17 in BCD.

Index register application – INDEX1

The following application is part of a system in which the contents of four data registers D20–D23 can be displayed, one after another, each time an input (X3) occurs.

This could be used in a stock control system, in which four different components are constantly being put into and removed from a storage area.

A bar-code reader might be used to record the transfer of the components to and from the storage area and feed the information into the PLC. Such a system would enable constant monitoring of the stock levels of the four components.

The project INDEX1 is much more simplified, in that the stock levels are fixed data values within the program.

Ladder diagram – INDEX1

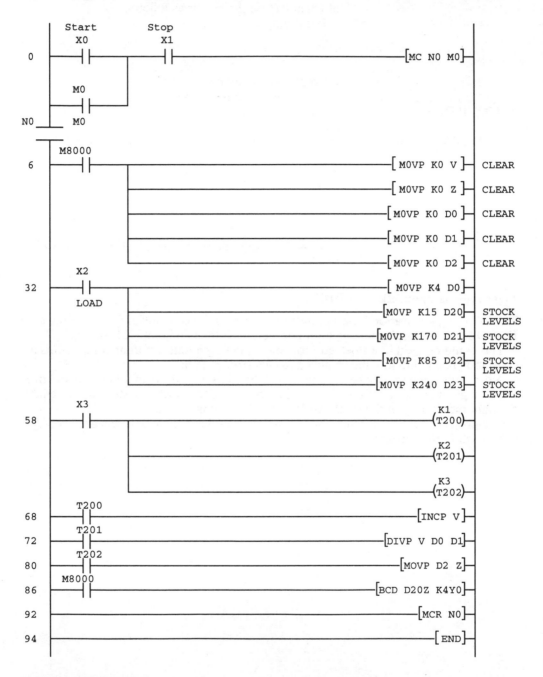

Principle of operation

1. Line 0
   The operation of the start button X0, enables M0 to latch and the remaining instructions to become operative, via the M0 master contact.

2. Line 6
The M8000 contact is closed while the PLC is in RUN. This ensures that on the first operation of the circuit, the following registers are reset:
(a) V
(b) Z
(c) D0
(d) D1
(e) D2
3. Line 32
The operation of input X2 causes constant values to be loaded into the following registers:
(a) Data Register D0
This register contains the total number of registers used to store data (i.e. 4).
(b) Data Registers D20–D23
These four registers are the ones used for storing the actual data (i.e. the stock levels):

D20 = 15
D21 = 170
D22 = 85
D23 = 240

4. Line 58
The operation of input X3 enables three 0.01 s pulses, T200, T201 and T202, to be generated one after the other. This ensures that, the circuit will operate in the correct sequence and enable the contents of the data registers D20, D21, D22 and D23 to be displayed sequentially.
5. Line 68
Each time T200 closes, this will cause index register V to be incremented.
6. Line 72
Each time T201 closes, this will cause the contents of index register V to be divided by the contents of D0 (i.e. 4).
(a) The dividend is stored in D1.
(b) The remainder, which must be a value in the range 0 to 3, is stored in D2.

	Division results – V/4		
V	Quotient (D1)	Remainder (D2)	
0	0	0	
1	0	1	
2	0	2	Range of numbers in D2
3	0	3	
4	1	0	
5	1	1	
6	1	2	
7	1	3	
8	2	0	
.	.	.	
.	.	.	
.	.	.	

7. Line 80
   Each time T202 closes, the contents of D2 (0–3) are loaded into index register Z.
8. Line 86
   The contents of the selected data register (i.e. D20–D23) are now displayed on the Y outputs Y0–Y7 in BCD format. The actual register selected, is dependent on the contents of the index register Z.
10. Hence, each time input X3 is operated, the contents of data registers D20, D21, D22 and D23 will be displayed sequentially.

Monitoring – INDEX1

Using decimal device monitoring, monitor the following:

1. X2
2. X3
3. D0
4. D1
5. D2
6. D20
7. D21
8. D22
9. D23
10. V
11. Z
12. K4Y0

18.4   Sub-routines

A Sub-routine is a separate section of a ladder diagram, which carries out a specific task and which is usually placed after the main section. The sub-routine is called from a known part of the main program using the instruction CALL.

Once the Sub-routine instructions have been executed then the execution of the instruction SRET causes the program to return to the main section and execute the instructions immediately following the instruction CALL.

The diagram on the facing page shows that the main program consists simply of three calls to three different sub-routines.

Sub-routine program flow

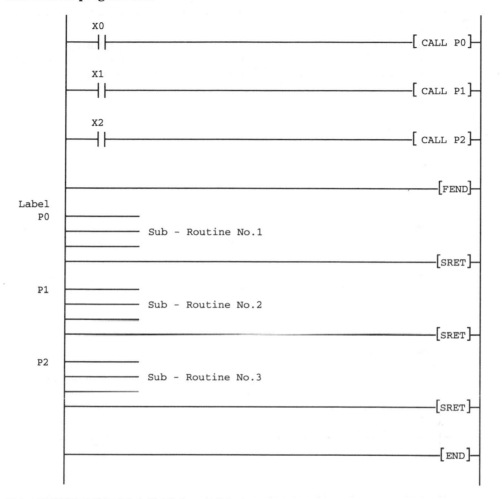

Principle of operation

1. When input X0 is ON, the execution of the CALL instruction will cause a jump to the first group of subroutine instructions, which start at label P0.
2. The sub-routine instructions are now executed until the sub-routine return (SRET) instruction is executed.
3. The program will now return to the main program, to enable the remaining main program instructions to be executed, or as shown on the diagram above, to call the next sub-routine.

Note

In the earlier versions of the FX PLC, 64 labels are available, in the range P0–P63. The 3.3 version has a total of 128 labels in the range P0–P127.

At the end of the main program instructions there must be an instruction FEND, to designate the end of the main program. This ensures that only the main program instructions will be executed, when there is no CALL to a sub-routine.

SUB1

The program SUB1 is used to demonstrate the use of a sub-routine within a ladder diagram program.

The main part of the program is used to input, via X0–X7, a temperature in the range 0 to 99°C. The sub-routine part of the program then converts the temperature to degrees Fahrenheit. The formula for converting degrees centigrade to degrees Fahrenheit is:

$$°F = (°C × 9/5) + 32$$

Ladder diagram – SUB1

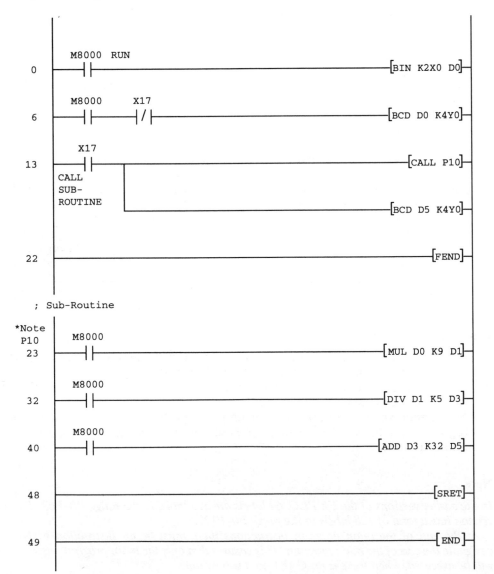

Note

Labels are in the range from P0 to P127.

A label is entered at the point on the ladder diagram by initially entering key 9 P,I. A small window then appears, into which the label (i.e. P10, < ent >) can be entered.

Principle of operation – SUB1

1. Line 0
   The 8 bit contents of X0–X7, which is the input temperature in degrees centigrade, are copied in BCD format to data register D0.
2. Line 6
   The temperature in degrees centigrade is now displayed on the outputs Y0–Y17 in BCD format.
3. Line 13
   The operation of input X17 enables the following:
   (a) The call to the sub-routine at label P10.
   (b) The sub-routine enables the input temperature to be converted from degrees centigrade to degrees Fahrenheit.
   (c) The display of the converted temperature in degrees Fahrenheit on the same outputs, Y0–Y17.
4. Line 22
   The instruction FEND terminates the main section of the program.
5. Line 23
   This is the start of the sub-routine section of the program at label P10. The first instruction of the sub-routine multiplies C by 9 and stores the result in data registers D1 and D2.
6. Line 32
   The contents of D1 are now divided by 5 and the result stored in data registers D3 and D4.
7. Line 40
   Finally the constant value of 32 is added to the contents of D3 and the result is stored in data register D5.
   Data Register D5 now contains the converted value in degrees Fahrenheit.
8. Line 48
   The instruction SRET returns the program back to the main section, and executes the instruction immediately following the instruction CALL. This instruction is –[BCD D5 K4Y0]–, which displays the converted temperature in degrees Fahrenheit.

Monitoring

Using Decimal Device Monitoring, monitor the following:

1. K2X0
2. D0
3. D1
4. D3
5. D5
6. K4Y0

Check

1. 0 degrees centigrade is equivalent to 32 degrees Fahrenheit.
2. 99 degrees centigrade is equivalent to 210 degrees Fahrenheit.

18.5 Interrupts

An interrupt is an input signal, which halts the execution of the main program and then immediately jumps to an interrupt service routine (ISR). The ISR carries out a specific task and then returns to the main program.

However, the main difference between an interrupt and a sub-routine CALL is that an interrupt can occur at any time during the execution of the main program, whereas a sub-routine CALL can only be carried out when, during the scan time of the main program, the instruction CALL is executed.

If it is necessary to take immediate action in the event of a particular input signal being operated, then the use of an interrupt should be considered. However, if immediate action were required in the event of an emergency stop situation, then safety relays, as described on pages 101–4, must be used and not the operation of an interrupt input.

Interrupt program – PNEU4

The following ladder diagram, is an example of how an interrupt can be used with a sequential PLC control program.

Note

The interrupt signal in this program is the operation of input X0.

The basis of this interrupt program is that the PLC is connected to a data logger computer and at regular intervals the computer generates an interrupt signal, by operating input X0. The PLC then sends back on the Y outputs, the number of complete machine cycles which have occurred since the previous interrupt signal was generated. The computer could for example, then produce the following management information:

1. The number of components produced in a given time.
2. The reliability of the machine. That is, has any production time been lost due to breakdowns?
3. The total operating time of the machine and, from this information, the determination of when required maintenance procedures should be carried out.

Interrupt program – PNEU4

Main program

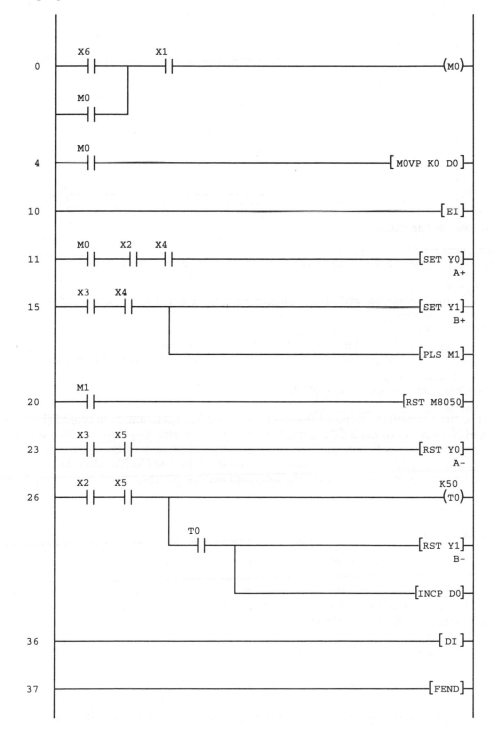

Interrupt service routine

Principle of operation

Main program
The main program functions almost exactly as PNEU2 except the following.

1. Line 26
   Each time a complete cycle has been carried out, the contents of data register D0 are incremented by one.
2. Lines 10–36
   The conditions for an interrupt to be accepted are as follows:
   (a) The interrupt must occur between the instructions EI (Enable Interrupt) and DI (Disable Interrupt).
   (b) The special memory coil M8050 must not SET.
3. Line 20
   Resetting M8050 at this point ensures that an interrupt can only be accepted after X3 and X4 have both been ON simultaneously (i.e. A+ and B–). This ensures that an interrupt can only be accepted once, during one complete machine cycle.
4. After five complete cycles, press the interrupt input button (X0), so that the program will immediately start executing the interrupt service routine.

Interrupt service routine

1. Line 38
   The contents of data register D0 are transferred to the outputs Y10–Y17 in BCD format. The contents of D0 are then cleared.
   Memory Coil M8050 is now SET. This ensures that the ISR can only be operative once per machine cycle. This is necessary because if the X0 input is still ON when the ISR is completed, then when the program returns to the main program, the interrupt will immediately be re-enabled.
2. Label I001
   (a) The label I001 is obtained as follows:

I	0	0	1
Interrupt	X0	No Meaning	Interrupt occurs on a positive-going signal. X0 turning ON

   (b) Only six interrupt inputs, X0–X5, are available on the FX series of PLCs.

3. Line 52

The execution of the interrupt return –[IRET]– instruction indicates that the ISR has been completed and the program can return to the main program.

Wiring diagram – PNEU4

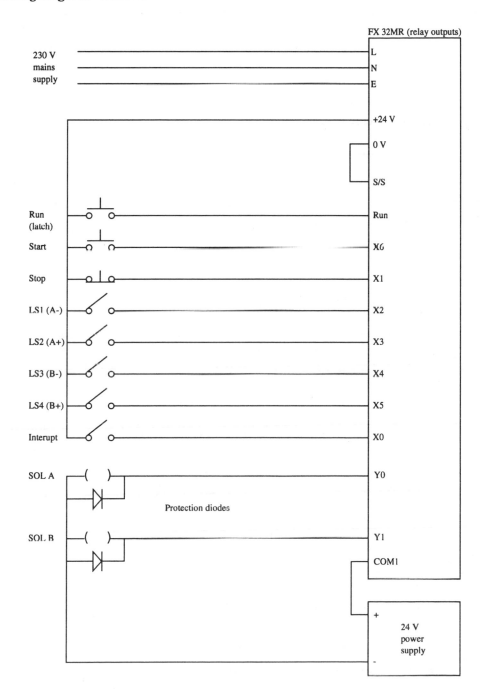

Monitoring – PNEU4

Let the pneumatic panel run automatically for five complete cycles and during the sixth cycle operate the interrupt button X0.

Using Decimal Device Monitoring, monitor the following:

1. M0 Start
2. X0 Interrupt input
3. X2 A–
4. X3 A+
5. X4 B–
6. X5 B+
7. Y0 Piston A
8. Y1 Piston B
9. D0 Cycles completed counter

19
Industrial application projects

The projects which will be developed in this chapter are based on applications, which could be used in industry. The projects which will be covered are as follows

1. SHIFT2   Quality control packaged cornflakes.
2. CENTRE1   Centring of scrap metal bars.
3. DIAGNOS1   Diagnostic monitoring.
4. QUEUE1   Queuing system – injection moulding machines

19.1 Quality control – SHIFT2

Scenario

Imagine a situation in which eight boxes on a conveyor system have just been filled with cornflakes and it is necessary to check as part of the quality control system within the plant that the boxes have been filled to the correct level.

The boxes now move rightwards eight places until they are located beneath eight sonic-level detectors. It is necessary to use eight sensors, since the measuring time per sensor is quite long and the use of this number of sensors effectively reduces the measurement time by a factor of 8.

• If the height of the cornflakes within the box is correct

$$\text{sensor output} = \text{logic } 0.$$

• Else as height is incorrect

$$\text{sensor output} = \text{logic } 1.$$

The output from the detectors is now transferred to the shift register via inputs X7–X0.

After the first box position there is a pneumatic ejector, which will eject a box from the conveyor belt, if the measured level of the cornflakes within that box is below the required level.

Each box now moves one place right and at the same time the contents of the shift register also move one place right. That is, the shift register is being used to 'track' the boxes as they move along the conveyor belt. Whenever there is a logic 1 in the carry (M8022) of the shift register, then that box will be rejected, since it has not been filled to the correct level.

Block diagram – sonic measuring system

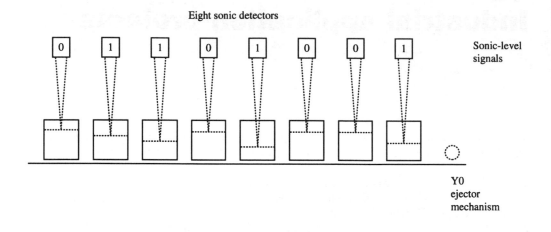

Eight sonic detectors

Sonic-level signals

Y0
ejector
mechanism

Shift register instruction ROR

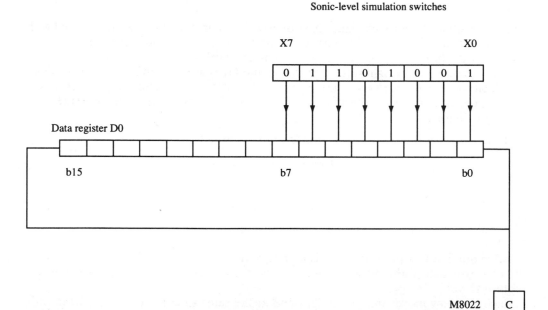

Sonic-level simulation switches

Using the instruction - [MOV K2X0 D0] -, the 8 bit contents of inputs X0–X7 are transferred to bits b0–b7 of the 16 bit data register D0. Each time a shift pulse occurs, the contents of D0 are rotated one place right and the contents of the lsb bit 0 are shifted into the carry flag M8022.

Ladder diagram – SHIFT2

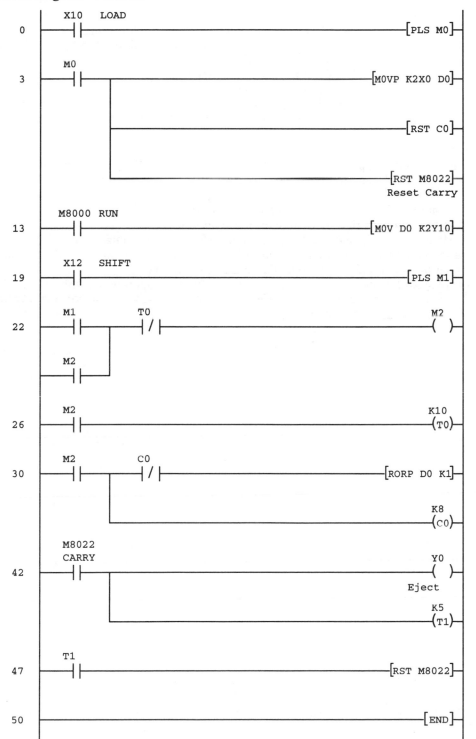

Principle of operation – SHIFT2

1. Lines 0–3

   The operation of input X10 pulses M0, which enables the following to occur:

   (a) The 8 bit data from X0–X7, which is simulating the levels of cornflakes within the eight boxes, is loaded into data register D0.

   (b) The counter C0 is reset to zero. This counter is used to ensure that only eight shift pulses can be generated for each block of data, input from X0–X7.

   (c) The carry or overflow flag M8022 is also reset to zero. Each time a shift right pulse is generated, the logic state of the LSB bit 0, is transferred both to this flag and to the msb bit 15 of the shift register.

2. Line 19

   The instruction -[MOV D0 K2Y10]- is used to enable the contents of the shift register to be constantly monitored on the outputs Y10–Y17.

3. Lines 22–26

   The input X12 simulates the movement of the conveyor. These input pulses are used to initiate the shift right pulse circuit of M2 and T0.

   Memory coil M2 and the 1 second timer T0 are used to ensure that a shift right pulse can only be generated at a rate of one per second, irrespective of the rate at which the input X12 is operated. This ensures the following:

   (a) Any switch bounce of input X12 will not affect the operation of the system.

   (b) There is sufficient time for a reject box to be ejected from the conveyor, before the arrival of the next conveyor pulse.

4. Shift register waveforms

It can be seen from the waveforms below that the maximum rate for the shift register pulse (X12) is one per second.

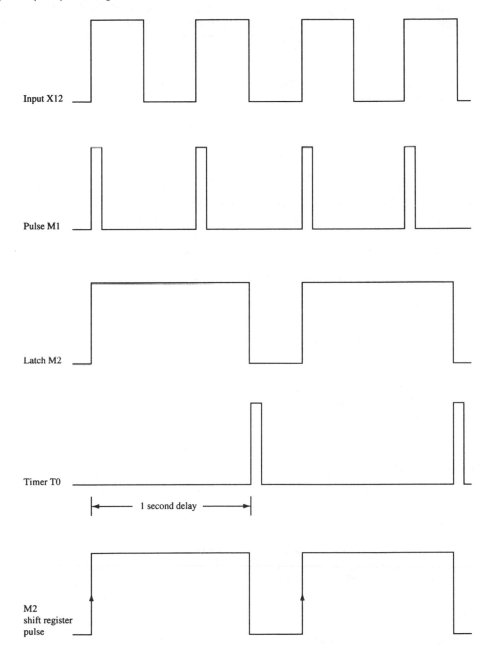

Input X12

Pulse M1

Latch M2

Timer T0

1 second delay

M2
shift register
pulse

5. Line 30

Each time a shift pulse occurs, the 16 bit contents of data register D0 are rotated one place to the right and the contents of the lsb bit 0, are shifted into the carry flag M8022.

At the same time the contents of counter C0 are incremented by one. After eight shift pulses counter C0 will operate, which indicates the following:

(a) The last box in each batch has moved off the conveyor system and hence it is necessary to prevent additional shift pulses occurring, until the next batch is in place. This ensures that the shift register contents cannot be shifted right more than eight times for every 8 bit block of input data.

(b) A new block of data has to be input from X0–X7.

6. Line 42
   When a logic 1 is shifted into the carry flag M8022, then this will initiate the box ejection circuit of timer T1 and output Y0.

   The closure of the M8022 contact will energize output Y0, which is used to eject the incorrectly filled box and also to energize the coil of timer T1.

7. Line 47
   After the 0.5 seconds delay of timer T1, the closure of its normally open contacts will reset the carry flag M8022 and hence de-energize output Y0.

8. After the batch of eight boxes has moved off the conveyor belt, there will be a new batch of eight boxes, whose contents will now be measured.

   Operating X10 (line 0) will enable the process to be repeated.

Monitoring – SHIFT2

Using Decimal Device Monitoring, monitor the following elements:

1. K2X0   The 8 bit Inputs, which simulate if the cornflake boxes have been correctly filled.
2. X10   The input data signal.
3. X12   The shift register pulse.
4. D0   The shift register.
5. C0   The shift register counter.
6. T0   The shift register pulse timer.
7. T1   The ejection timer.
8. M8022 The carry flag.
9. Y0

Setup procedure

1. Operate all the input switches X0 to X7. This will produce the binary pattern 1111 1111.
2. Operate the input X10 to load the input switch information into data register D0.
3. Operate the shift input X12 six times.
4. The Decimal Device Monitor, will be as shown below.
5. Since all of the cornflake boxes have been incorrectly filled, output Y0 will operate for 0.5 seconds each time a shift pulse (X12) is applied.

Monitor display

The monitor display on the facing page shows the following:

1. Input K2X0 is hexadecimal FF, that is all eight boxes have been incorrectly filled.
2. The shift register has been shifted right six times, that is counter C0 = 6.

```
Working Area              Offline    SHIFT2            FX          Ladder
Find     Save    Name     Copy       Move     Delete   Exchange    Test
Step     I/o     Text
Monitor  Decimal
```

```
------------------------- Device Monitor -------------------------
I/O      Name    Decimal   Pre/ASC   Hex    FEDC   BA98   7654   3210

K2X0             255                 FF                   1111   1111
X10              0                   0                           0
X12              0                   0                           0
D0               -1021     n♥        FC03   1111   1100   0000   0011
C0               6         K8        6      0000   0000   0000   0110
T0               0         K10       0      0000   0000   0000   0000
T1               0                   0      0000   0000   0000   0000
M8022            1         ☺ 1       1                    1
Y0               1         ☺ 1       1                    1
```

Note

M8022 and output Y0 will return to a logic 0 after 0.5 seconds, that is when timer T1 times out.

19.2 Centring of scrap metal bars

Centring system – CENTRE1

The following application requires that the centre of a scrap metal bar be determined, irrespective of the length of the bar. This is done so that the bar can be lifted from its centre by an electromagnet hoist system. The bar is then moved and lowered into a furnace, where it can be melted and hence recycled. If the hoist did not lift the bar from its centre, then the bar would tip over as it was being lifted.

Centring system diagram

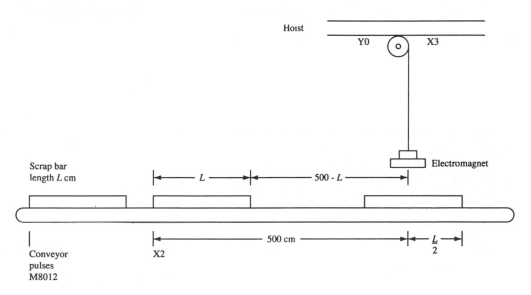

Basic operation

1. As the conveyor belt moves, it outputs pulses, which are used to indicate the distance the conveyor, and hence the distance each scrap bar, has travelled.
2. To simulate these pulses, special auxiliary relay M8012 is used to output a pulse once every 0.1 seconds. Each pulse simulates a movement of 1 centimetre.
3. The 1 second pulses are output to Y3, to indicate the conveyor is operating.
4. When the leading edge of the scrap bar reaches the limit switch X2, the pulses from M8012 are counted by data register D0.
5. When the trailing edge of the scrap bar clears limit switch X2, then the count in D0 is transferred to data register D1, where the contents are then divided by 2. This is done to obtain a measurement, equal to one-half of the bar's length.

   The distance still to be travelled by the bar after it has cleared the limit switch X2, is $500 - L/2$ cm.
6. The bar continues towards the centre of the electromagnet and for each centimetre of movement, the contents of data register D1 are incremented by one.
7. When the contents of D1 reach the value of 500, that is the distance in centimetres from X2 to the electromagnet, then the centre of the bar, irrespective of its length, will be directly under the electromagnet.
8. When this occurs (i.e. D1 = 500), output Y0 is energised causing the conveyor to stop and the hoist sequence to start. On completion of the hoist sequence, input X3 is operated to restart the sequence.

Mathematical analysis

1. Whilst the bar is operating input X2, data register D0 is counting the simulated conveyor 0.1 second pulses from M8012.

   Let the pulse rate be n pulses per cm. When the bar clears X2, the contents of D0 are halved.
2. Hence the number of pulses whilst X2 is made is $L \times n/2$.
3. The additional number of pulses until the leading edge of the bar reaches the centre of the hoist is $(500 - L) \times n$.
4. The additional number of pulses until the centre of the bar is directly under the hoist is $L/2 \times n$
5. Total number of pulses in data register D1 is

$$D1 = L \times n/2 + (500 - L) \times n + L/2 \times n$$
$$= L \times n/2 + 500 \times n - L \times n + L/2 \times n$$
$$= L \times n + 500 \times n - L \times n$$
$$= 500 \times n$$

6. Hence it can be seen that when the value in D1 reaches $500 \times n$, the centre of the metal bar will be directly under the centre of the hoist, irrespective of the length of the bar.
7. In simulating the system, n is equivalent to one pulse every centimetre.
8. Hence the value in D1 equals 500.

   When the value in D1 reaches 500, the centre of the bar is directly under the centre of the electromagnet.
9. The total distance travelled by any bar of length L, so that it is centralized under the electromagnet, will be $500 + L/2$ cm.

Ladder diagram – CENTRE1

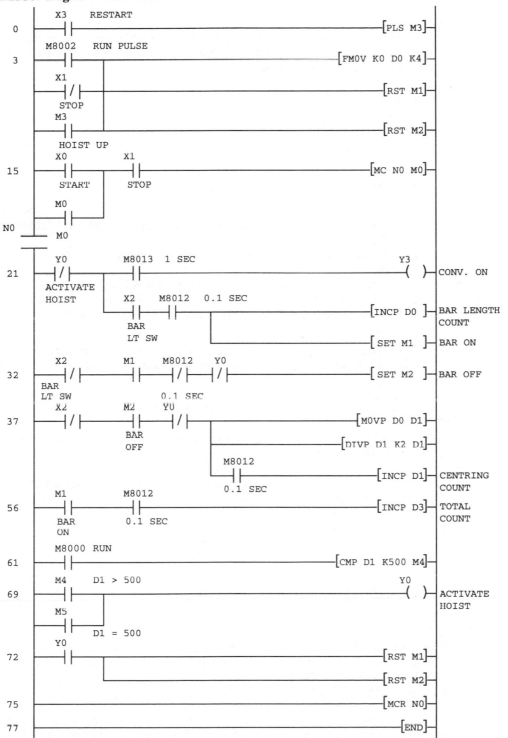

Principle of operation – CENTRE1

1. Line 0
   The operation of input X3 simulates a signal from the hoist that it is in the UP position and ready to start another sequence. With input X3 operating, this will cause M3 to be pulsed ON, for one scan time.
2. Line 3
   (a) Let any one of the following be operated.
       (i)   M8002   The one-shot RUN pulse.
       (ii) X1   The stop input.
       (iii) M3   The repeat sequence signal, caused by the operation of input X3.
   (b) The operation of any one of the above will execute the following instructions:
       (i)   FMOV K0 D0 K4.
             This will clear the four data registers D0–D3.

             D0   Is used to count the simulated conveyor pulses whilst the bar is operating the input X2. Hence the final count in D0 is the length of the bar in centimetres.
             D1   Is used to count the total number of pulses required to centralize the bar.
             D2   Is used as the remainder when $-[D1VP\ D1\ K2\ D1]-$ is executed.
             D3   Is used to count the total number of simulated conveyor pulses, which, in turn, enables a check to be made on the accuracy of the system.

       (ii) RST M1
             This ensures that when the PLC is first switched to RUN, or the Stop Cycle input X1 is pressed, then M1, the BAR ON memory, is reset.
       (iii) RST M2
             This also ensures that when the PLC is first switched to RUN, or the Stop Cycle input X1 is pressed, then M2, the BAR OFF memory, is reset.
3. Line 15
   Inputs X0 and X1 are the inputs to a standard start and stop cycle latch circuit, which uses the master contact instruction $-[MC\ N0\ M0]-$.
4. Line 21
   (a) The normally closed contact of Y0 indicates that, as yet, no start signal has been sent to the hoist, to activate its operation.
       The output Y0 is used to indicate that a bar has been centralized.
   (b) The 1 second pulses of M8013 are used to turn the output Y3 ON/OFF, which, in turn, are used to indicate the operation of the conveyor.
   (c) When a bar operates the limit switch X2, then 0.1 second pulses from M8012 are used to increment D0.
       The first pulse of M8012 after the operation of X2 is used to set M1. This is used to indicate that the leading edge of the bar has operated the limit switch X2.
5. Line 32
   (a) When the bar clears the X2 limit switch, input X2 will remake. This, plus the setting of M1, the next falling edge of M8012, and the normally closed contact of Y0, will cause M2 to be set.
   (b) The operation of M2 also indicates that the bar has $500 - L/2$ cm still to travel.
6. Line 37
   The operation of M2 (i.e. when the bar clears input X2) causes the following to occur:
   (a) The count stored in D0, which is the length of the bar, is transferred to D1.

(b) The contents of D2 are divided by 2, with the quotient stored back into D2 and the remainder (i.e. a zero or a one, stored in D3.

(c) While the bar carries on travelling towards the electromagnet, the pulses increment D1.

7. Line 56

From the instant when the leading edge of the bar operates the limit switch X2, and hence sets M1, the total number of pulses will be counted by D3. This count will be used later to verify the accuracy of the system.

8. Line 61

When the count stored in D1 reaches 500, the comparison instruction will operate M5:

M4 ON, if D1 > 500.
M5 ON, if D1 = 500.
M6 ON, if D1 < 500.

9. With the operation of M5, the bar is centralized under the electromagnet and Y0 is energized to send a signal to the hoist.

The hoist now lowers the electromagnet on to the centre of the bar. The electromagnet is turned ON and the bar is lifted and transported to the furnace.

10. Line 72

With the operation of Y0, the BAR ON memory M1 and the BAR OFF memory M2 are reset.

Monitoring – CENTRE1

Using decimal device monitoring, monitor the following elements:
1. X0   Start cycle.
2. X1   Stop cycle.
3. X2   Bar limit switch.
4. M0   Master contact memory.
5. M1   BAR ON memory.
6. M2   BAR OFF memory.
7. M4   D1 > 500.
8. M5   D1 = 500.
9. M6   D1 < 500.
10. D0   Bar length counter.
11. D1   Centralizing counter.
12. D2   Remainder.
13. D3   Totalizing counter.
14. Y0   Activate hoist signal.

Setup procedure

1. Initially, ensure that all inputs X0–X3 are OFF.
2. Operate the Stop cycle switch X1 and then press the Start cycle push button X0.
3. The Y3 output will start pulsing ON/OFF every second, indicating that the conveyor is operating.
4. Using Decimal Device Monitoring, monitor the elements listed above.
5. Operate the bar limit switch X2 and note that the contents of D0 and D3 are being incremented.

6. When D0 reaches approximately 100, turn X2 OFF.
7. D0 will stop incrementing, but now D1 will start incrementing along with D3.
8. When D1 reaches 500, M5 will operate, as will the Output Y0. Also, the simulated operation of the conveyor (i.e. the 1 second pulsing of Y3) will stop.
9. Note the contents of D0, D1 and D3.
10. To restart the sequence, momentarily operate the Restart input X3 and repeat from item 5.

Monitoring

The display below is of the decimal device monitor for CENTRE1.

Working	Area			Offline	CENTRE1			FX		Ladder
Find	Save	Name		Copy	Move		Delete	Exchange		Test
Step	I/o	Text								

Monitor   Decimal

────────────────── Device Monitor ──────────────────

I/O	Name	Decimal	Pre/ASC	Hex	FEDC	BA98	7654	3210
X0		0		0				0
X1		1	☺	1				1
X2		0	☺	0				0
M0		1	☺	1				1
M1		0		0				0
M2		0		0				0
M3		0		0				0
M4		0		0				0
M5		1	☺	1				1
D0		100	d	64	0000	0000	0110	0110
D1		500	☺⌐	1F4	0000	0001	1111	0100
D2		0		0	0000	0000	0000	0000
D3		550	☺&	226	0000	0010	0010	0111
Y0		1	☺	1				1

Verification of results

From the above monitoring details it can be seen that the length of the bar L, as measured by D0, is 100 cm. The total distance travelled by the bar (td) is:

$$td = 500 + L/2$$

This is measured by the count in D3. Therefore

D3 = 500 + D0/2
D3 = 500 + 100/2
D3 = 550

This shows that the total distance a 100 cm bar has to travel so that it is centralized under the electromagnet is 550 cm.

CENTRE2

Example 4 on page 217 requires an alarm to be incorporated for when the length of a metal bar exceeds 500 cm.

19.3 Diagnostic fault finding – DIAGNOS1

Scenario – DIAGNOS1

A manufacturing machine, which is controlled by a PLC, stops intermittently during its automatic cycle. The problem appears to be that if five input limit switches X0–X4 do not operate sequentially one after another within a time period of 8 seconds, this will cause the machine to stop.

The program DIAGNOS1 is used to diagnose that when a fault condition does occur, the following information is available to the maintenance engineers:

1. Did the limit switches operate within the 8 second period?
2. Did the limit switches operate in the correct order (i.e. X0, X1, X2, X3, X4)?
3. The times at which the limit switches operated.

Ladder diagram – DIAGNOS1

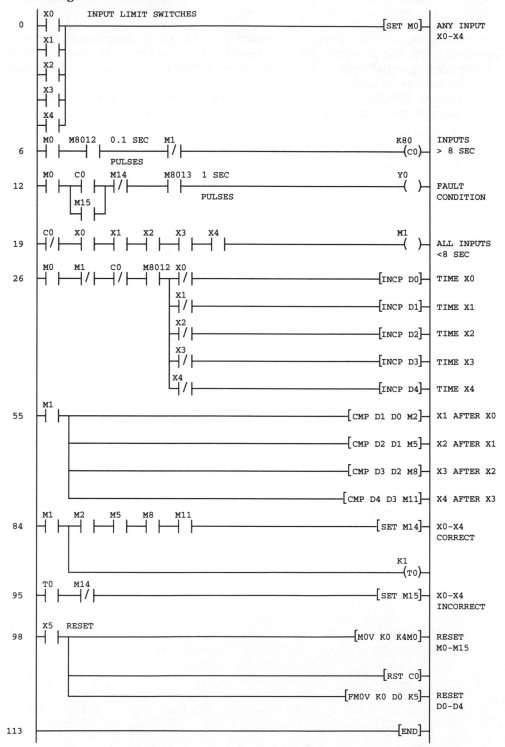

Principle of operation – DIAGNOS1

1. Line 0
   The operation of any one of the inputs X0–X4 will energize M0.
2. Line 6
   (a) As soon as the first input operates, then 0.1 second pulses are fed to the counter C0.
   (b) If M1 operates before C0 has reached its maximum count of 80, then all of the inputs have operated in less than 8 seconds.
   (c) However, if counter C0 does operate, then not all of the inputs have operated within the required 8 seconds.
3. Line 12
   (a) If the C0 contacts close, then this is a fault condition and hence the output Y0 will flash ON/OFF at 1 second intervals.
   (b) It will be shown later that if M15 operates, this is also a fault condition.
4. Line 19
   The auxiliary memory M1 will only operate if all of the inputs X0–X4 operate within the required time of 8 seconds.
5. Line 26
   (a) Provided that neither M1 nor C0 has operated, then on the operation of the first input limit switch, 0.1 second pulses will be applied simultaneously to four out of the five data registers, D0–D4.
   (b) The one data register which does not count up will be the one which is connected to the normally closed contacts of the input, which operated first of all.
   (c) For example, if input X0 operates first of all, then its normally closed contacts will open and hence data register D0 will be unable to count up.
   (d) The remaining data registers will now count up every 0.1 seconds, until the input connected to each data register operates and opens the corresponding normally closed contact.
   (e) Therefore the values stored in the five data registers D0–D4 are the times in 0.1 seconds from the operation of the first input.
6. Line 55
   (a) If input M1 has operated (i.e. all of the inputs have operated within 8 seconds) then the next block of instructions will determine the order in which the inputs operated.
   (b) This is done by comparing the times at which the inputs actually operated.
   (c) For example, if input X0 operated first of all, then the value in its data register D0 will be 0.
   (d) Provided input X1 operated after X0, the value in D1 will be greater than 0, and therefore the first comparison, CMP D1 D0 M2, will operate M2.
      If X1 operated after X0, then D1 > D0. Hence M2 ON.
   (e) Similary if the value in D2 is greater than D1, then input X2 operated after input X1 and therefore M5 will operate.
      If X2 operated after X1, then D2 > D1. Hence M5 ON.
   (f) If X3 operated after X2, then D3 > D2. Hence M8 ON.
   (g) If X4 operated after X3, then D4 > D3. Hence M11 ON.
7. Line 84
   (a) After M1 has operated, the results of the four comparison instructions are stored in the memory coils M2–M13.
      Provided that the inputs X0–X4 have all operated one after another within 8 seconds, then the memory coils M2, M5, M8 and M11 will have operated, which in turn will have enabled M14 to operate.

(b) The operation of M14 indicates that the system is operating correctly.

(c) When M1 operated, it also started the 0.1 second timer T0. This is used to ensure that all the comparison instructions will have been scanned, executed and the results of the comparisons stored in the appropriate memory coils, before the timer times out.

8. Line 95

(a) If timer T0 times out and M14 has not operated, then M15 will operate.

(b) The operation of M15 indicates that the system is not operating correctly and hence there is a fault condition within the system.

9. Line 12

The operation of M15 will now cause the output Y0 to flash ON/OFF at 1 second intervals.

10. Line 98

Provided that the machine completes its automatic cycle with no problems occurring, then at the end of the cycle input X5 will operate, to reset the following:

(a) MOV K0 K4M0

This will reset all of the memory coils M0–M15.

(b) RST C0

This will reset the counter C0, which is used to obtain the 8 second window and within which all of the inputs X0–X4 must operate.

(c) FMOV K0 D0 K5

This will reset to zero the contents of the 5 data registers D0–D4, which are used to store the individual times when the inputs X0–X4 operated.

Monitoring – DIAGNOS1

Using Decimal Device Monitoring, the project DIAGNOS1 is now monitored under the following conditions:

1. When the system is operating correctly, that is all input limit switches operate in the correct order X0–X4 within 8 seconds.
2. Not all of the inputs operate within 8 seconds.
3. All of the inputs operate within 8 seconds, but not in the correct order.

Decimal device monitoring

Using Decimal Device Monitoring, monitor the following elements:

1. X0
2. X1
3. X2
4. X3
5. X4
6. C0
7. D0
8. D1
9. D2
10. D3
11. D4
12. M14
13. M15
14. Y0

Monitoring – condition 1

The monitor display shown below was obtained when the system was operating correctly.

Working	Area		Offline	DIAGNOS1		FX	Ladder
Find	Save	Name	Copy	Move	Delete	Exchange	Test
Step	I/o						

Monitor				Decimal				

Device Monitor

I/O	Name	Decimal	Pre/ASC	Hex	FEDC	BA98	7654	3210
X0		1	☺	1				1
X1		1	☺	1				1
X2		1	☺	1				1
X3		1	☺	1				1
X4		1	☺	1				1
C0		23	K80	17	0000	0000	0001	0001
D0		0		0	0000	0000	0000	0000
D1		6		6	0000	0000	0000	0110
D2		11		B	0000	0000	0000	1011
D3		17		11	0000	0000	0001	0001
D4		23	↕	17	0000	0000	0001	0111
M14		1	☺	1				1
M15		0		0				0
Y0		0		0				0

It can be seen from the monitor display that:

1. The values stored in D0–D4 are in ascending order. Therefore the inputs X0–X4 operated in the correct order.
2. The value in counter C0 is 23. Therefore all of the five inputs operated within 8 seconds.
3. M14 = 1. Therefore the system operated correctly.

Monitoring – condition 2

The monitor display shown below was obtained when not all of the inputs operated within 8 seconds.

Working	Area		Offline	DIAGNOS1		FX	Ladder
Find	Save	Name	Copy	Move	Delete	Exchange	Test
Step	I/o						

Monitor				Decimal				

Device Monitor

I/O	Name	Decimal	Pre/ASC	Hex	FEDC	BA98	7654	3210
X0		1	☺	1				1
X1		1	☺	1				1
X2		1	☺	1				1
X3		1	☺	1				1
X4		0		0				0
C0		80	K80	50	0000	0000	0101	0000
D0		0		0	0000	0000	0000	0000
D1		3		3	0000	0000	0000	0011
D2		12		C	0000	0000	0000	1100
D3		21		15	0000	0000	0001	0101
D4		79	O	4F	0000	0000	0100	1111
M14		0		0				0
M15		0		0				0
Y0		0/1		0/1				0/1

It can be seen from the monitor display that:

1. The values stored in D0–D4 are in ascending order, but the count in D4 is 79.
2. With counter C0 operating when its count is 80 and therefore its C0 contacts on line 26 opening, D4 is unable to count the 80th pulse or any further pulses due to input X4 not operating in time. In fact, by examining the display for X4, it can be seen that it did not operate at all.
3. Since C0 reached its maximum count of 80 owing to X4 not operating, this is a fault condition and output Y0 will flash ON/OFF.

Monitoring – condition 3

The monitor display shown below was obtained when all of the inputs operated within 8 seconds, but not in the correct order.

Working	Area		Offline	DIAGNOS1		FX	Ladder
Find	Save	Name	Copy	Move	Delete	Exchange	Test
Step	I/o						

Monitor				Decimal			

```
                          ── Device Monitor ──
  I/O    Name    Decimal   Pre/ASC    Hex    FEDC    BA98    7654    3210

  X0              1          ☺         1                                    1
  X1              1          ☺         1                                    1
  X2              1          ☺         1                                    1
  X3              1          ☺         1                                    1
  X4              1          ☺         1                                    1
  C0              56         K80        38     0000    0000    0011    1000
  D0              0                      0     0000    0000    0000    0000
  D1              56                    38     0000    0000    0011    1000
  D2              10                     A     0000    0000    0000    1010
  D3              15                    15     0000    0000    0001    0101
  D4              29         ↔          1D     0000    0000    0001    1101
  M14             0                      1                                  1
  M15             1          ☺          1                                  1
  Y0              0/1                   0/1                               0/1
```

It can be seen from the monitor display that:

1. The values stored in D0–D4 are not in ascending order. Therefore the inputs X0–X4 did not operate in the correct order.

    From the display it can be determined that the order in which the input switches operated was: X0, X2, X3, X4, X1.
2. The value in counter C0 = 56. Therefore all of the five inputs operated within 8 seconds.
3. M15 = 1, owing to the inputs not operating in the correct order. Since this is a fault condition, output Y0 will flash ON/OFF.

19.4 Automatic queuing system

This application is based on polycarbonate components being manufactured by five separate injection moulding machines.

The raw material is polycarbonate granules, which are stored in a central hopper and transferred to each machine's individual hopper by a vacuum system. Whenever one of the hopper's contents falls to a low value, then a signal is sent to the control system to enable the the required hopper to be topped up with granules. However, if the hopper is not filled up in time, and consequently its injection moulding machine has insufficient granules to produce the component, then this will cause production problems.

If a simple sequential filling control system were used, then by the very nature of its operation, problems would still occur. If, for example, while hopper 3 was being filled, hopper 1 became low, followed a short time later by hopper 5 also becoming low, then hopper 5 would be filled before hopper 1. This could mean that by the time hopper 1 is to be filled, it could already be empty.

To overcome this, should the hopper to one or more moulding machines fall low at the same time, or shortly after one another, a queuing system is used, which is based on the FIFO (First In – First Out) stack principle. This ensures that the order in which the requests are made will be identical to the order in which the granules are delivered to the hoppers and therefore, the granules in any of the individual hoppers will not be able to fall below a minimum acceptable level.

System hardware

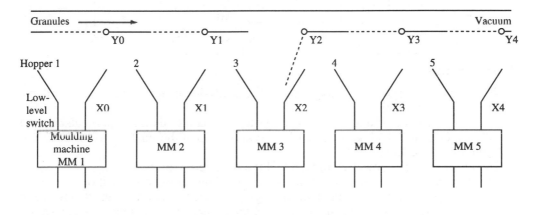

Manufactured components

PLC system software – QUEUE1

The PLC software is based on a five input queuing system in which five inputs X0–X5, are scanned in turn approximately every 0.1 seconds, and where an input is ON, its corresponding logical value is stored in a FIFO memory stack.

As each logical value is removed from the stack, it will cause the corresponding Y output to turn on for 30 seconds.

Input	Logical value k_L	Y output
X0	1	Y0
X1	2	Y1
X3	4	Y2
X4	8	Y3
X5	16	Y4

PLC software modules – QUEUE1

The block diagram below shows the major software modules required for the complete system.

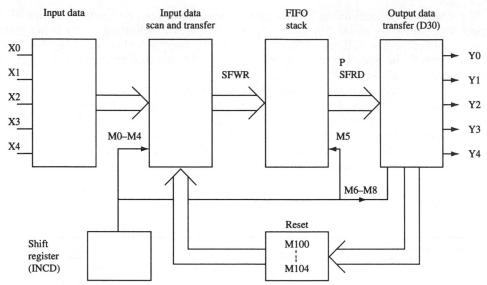

Basic operation

1. When an input is turned ON, its equivalent logical value is stored in the next available position on the FIFO stack.
2. After any one of the Y outputs has been ON for 30 seconds, then that particular output will turn OFF and the logical value which is at the top of the stack, is now transferred to the output section.
3. The logical value is now used to turn ON the required Y output.
4. At the same time, the contents of the stack are all moved up one position.
5. The operation continues until all of the logical values stored on the stack have been shifted out. This will occur if none of the X inputs are ON and hence no new values are being written to the stack.

Ladder diagram – QUEUE1

Shift register

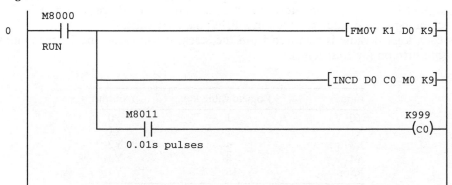

Input data scan and transfer

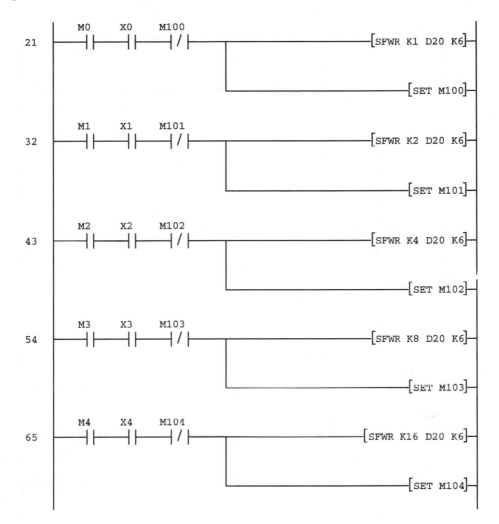

Output data transfer

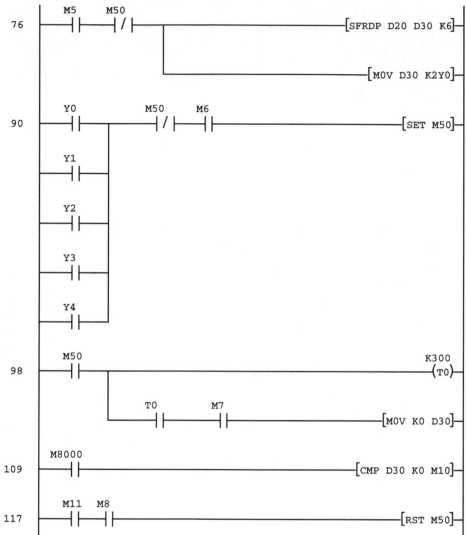

Reset

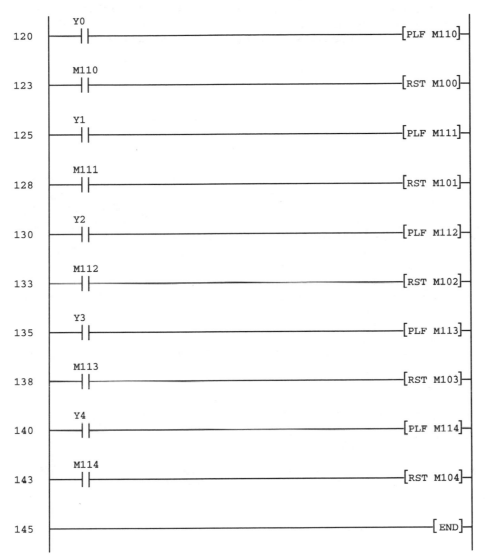

Principle of operation

1. Shift register
   Line 0
   (a) The shift register consists of nine memory coils M0—M8, which are sequentially turned ON for 0.01 seconds and then OFF for 0.08 seconds. The instruction which is used for this purpose is the incremental drum INCD.
   (b) Initially the data registers D0—D8 are all filled with the value of 1, using the instruction –[FMOV K1 D0 K9]–.
   (c) Each time the value in counter C0 reaches the value stored in each data register D0—D8 (i.e. a one, then the corresponding memory coil M0—M8, will turn ON. For example, when C0 reaches the value in D0 (i.e. a one), then M0 turns ON.

(d) Counter C0 is automatically reset and then starts recounting. When the value in C0 reaches the value in D1 (i.e. as before, a one), then M0 turns OFF and M1 turns ON.

(e) The process constantly repeats from M0 to M8 and then back to M0.

(f) The 0.01 second pulses from M8011 are used to increment C0.

Shift register waveforms

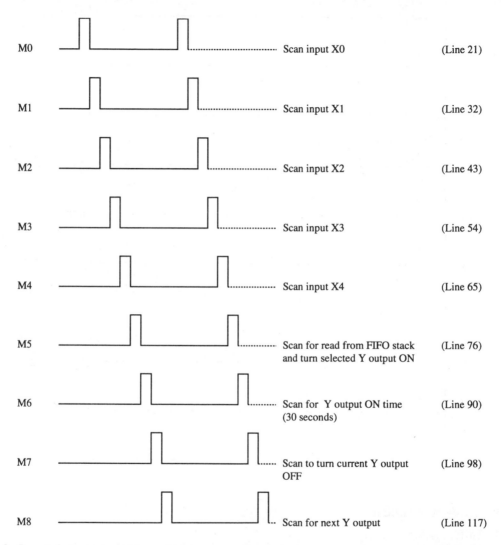

M0	Scan input X0	(Line 21)
M1	Scan input X1	(Line 32)
M2	Scan input X2	(Line 43)
M3	Scan input X3	(Line 54)
M4	Scan input X4	(Line 65)
M5	Scan for read from FIFO stack and turn selected Y output ON	(Line 76)
M6	Scan for Y output ON time (30 seconds)	(Line 90)
M7	Scan to turn current Y output OFF	(Line 98)
M8	Scan for next Y output	(Line 117)

2. Input data scan and transfer
   Lines 21–65
   (a) When any one of the inputs X0–X4 are turned on, then on being scanned by its corresponding shift register output, the logical value KL for that input is written to the FIFO Stack. This is done by using the using the shift write instruction -[SFWR KL D20 K6]-.
   (b) This instruction determines the following:
       (i)   The stack, will consist of six data registers D20 to D25.
       (ii) The stack pointer will be D20.

(iii) The stack registers which are to be used for storing the logical values, will be D21–D25.
(iv) When writing to the stack, it is the stack pointer's contents which are used to calculate which stack register will be used.
(v) For example, if D20 = 3, then stack register D(21+3) (i.e. D24) will be where the next logical value will be written to.
(vi) Each time a logical value is written to the stack, the stack pointer is incremented by one.
(c) Write stack format

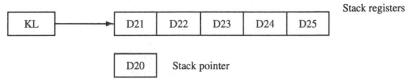

Stack registers

(d) Let the five X inputs be operated one after another in the following order:

Input	Logical value k_L
X0	1
X3	8
X1	2
X4	16
X5	4

(e) Line 21
With input X0 operating, its logical value (i.e. 1) will be written to D21 and the stack pointer D20 will be incremented to 1.
(f) Line 54
With input X3 operating, its logical value (i.e. 8) will be written to D22 and the stack pointer D20 will be incremented to 2.
(g) Line 32
Similary with input X1 operating, its Logical value (i.e. 2) will be written to D23 and the stack pointer D21 will be incremented to 03.
(h) Hence the data stored in the stack at this moment will be

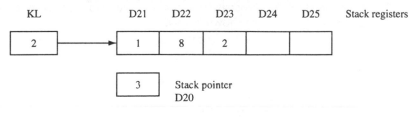

(i) Note that the next available stack register available for writing to is D24.
(j) The process continues until all of the five logical values have been stored on the stack.

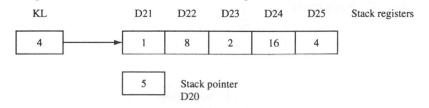

(k) Line 21
After the logical value for input X0 has been written to the stack, memory coil M100 is set and its associated normally closed contacts will open. This ensures that while the logical value corresponding to X0 is stored on the stack, then that same value cannot be rewritten to the stack, even if X0 stays operated. This facility therefore inhibits a logical value being written to the stack, while that value remains stored on the stack.

(l)

Line no	Stack inhibit memory
21	M100
32	M101
43	M102
54	M103
65	M104

3. FIFO Stack – Read
Line 76
(a) Data is read from the stack to data register D30 each time the instruction ‑[SFRDP D20 D30 K6]‑ is executed.
(b) Read Stack Format

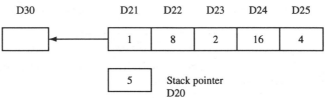

Line 76
(a) When the shift register contact M5 closes, and provided the contacts of timer T5O are also closed, the contents at the top of the stack (i.e. the contents of D21) are transferred to the data register D30.
(b) At the same time, the contents of the remaining stack registers are then shifted right one place and the contents of the stack pointer are decremented by one.
(c) The first time the stack read instruction ‑[SFRDP D20 D30 K6]‑ is executed, the contents of the stack will be as shown below.

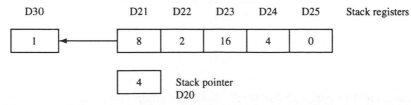

(d) The second time the stack read instruction is executed, the contents of the stack become as shown below.

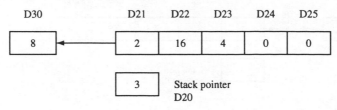

4. Output data transfer
   Line 76
   After the execution of each shift register read instruction, which transfers the logical value stored at the top of the Stack to D30, the output transfer instruction ⊣[MOV D30 K2Y0]⊢ is now executed. This enables the contents of data register D30 to be transferred to the actual Y outputs.

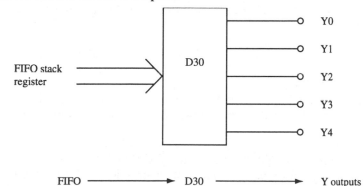

Output truth table
The Y outputs are turned ON, according to the following truth table.

Logical value	Binary Y4 Y3 Y2 Y1 Y0					Y output ON
01	0	0	0	0	1	Y0
02	0	0	0	1	0	Y1
04	0	0	1	0	0	Y2
08	0	1	0	0	0	Y3
16	1	0	0	0	0	Y4

Hence if the contents of D30 = 08, then output Y3 will turn ON.
5. Output – ON Time
   Lines 90–98
   When a Y output is turned ON, it is only ON for 30 seconds, this being sufficient time to fill an individual hopper with the polycarbonate granules.
   The following describes how this is done.
   (a) Line 90
       With the operation of any one of the five Y outputs, M50 will be set, when the shift register output M6 turns ON
   (b) Line 98
       (i)   The closing of the M50 contacts will start a 30 second time delay T0.
       (ii) At the end of the 30 seconds, the T0 contacts will close and with the operation of the shift register output M7, the instruction ⊣[MOV K0 D30]⊢ will be executed.
       (iii) This instruction clears the contents of D0 and on the next scan of the program, when the instruction ⊣[MOV D30 K2Y0]⊢ is executed (line 76), the Y output which is currently ON will be turned OFF.
6. Next Y Output
   (a) Line 109
       (i)   When a particular Y output has completed its hopper fill sequence, then it is necessary for the next Y output to be turned ON.

    (ii)   The logical value for the next Y output is currently at the top of the stack and hence the stack read instruction has now to be executed.

    (iii) With D30 being cleared at the end of the 30 second time period, a comparison is now made of the contents of D30, using the instruction ─[CMP D30 K0 M10]─.

(b) Line 117

    With D30 = 0, M11 will operate and this, plus the shift register output M8, will reset M50.

(c) Line 76

    (i)   With the closure of the M50 normally closed contacts, the stack read instruction SFRD D20 D30 K6, and the output transfer instruction MOV D30 K2Y0, will both be executed.

    (ii) This will enable the next logical value stored at the top of the stack, to be transferred to D30 and hence the next required Y output will be turned ON.

7. Reset

    Lines 120–123

(a) After an output (i.e. Y0) has been turned ON and then OFF, the normally open contact of Y0, will reopen to enable the instruction PLF M110 to be executed.

(b) PLF waveforms

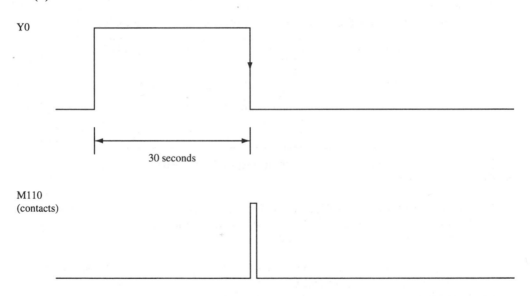

(c) On the falling edge of the Y0 contact, the instruction PLF 110 will be executed. This instruction causes the operation of M110 for one scan time (i.e. it is similar to PLS), but whereas PLS operates on the rising edge of an input (see page 77), PLF operates on the falling edge of an input.

(d) This in turn causes M110 to output a pulse for one scan time, which resets M100, the stack inhibit memory and re-enables the X0 circuit input in the input data scan and transfer section (line 21).

(e) Should X0 still be ON or come ON, then the transfer of the logical value corresponding to X0 will be reloaded back onto the stack.

    Lines 125–143

The other stack inhibit memories (i.e. M101, M102, M103 and M104) will also be reset when their corresponding Y output is turned OFF.

Testing the system

To test that the QUEUE1 system operates as specified, carry out the following:

1. Ensure all of the X inputs and the Y outputs are OFF.
2. Switch ON the X inputs in the following order and leave them switched ON: X0, X3, X1, X4, X2.
3. The Y outputs will now come ON one at a time, every 30 seconds, in the following order: Y0, Y3, Y1, Y4, Y2.
4. The cycle will repeat itself until the X inputs are switched OFF, or the RUN is switched OFF.

Monitoring the stack contents

Using Decimal Device Monitoring, monitor the contents of the stack as follows.

Procedure

1. Ensure that all of the X inputs and the Y outputs are OFF.
2. Switch ON the X inputs in the following order and then turn them all OFF:

X0, X3, X1, X4, X2.

3. The display shown below, is at the instant when the output Y3 is ON.

Working Area			Offline	QUEUE1		FX	Ladder
Find	Save	Name	Copy	Move	Delete	Exchange	Test
Step	I/o						

Monitor					Decimal			

```
                          ─── Device Monitor ───
  I/O    Name    Decimal    Pre/ASC    Hex    FEDC    BA98    7654    3210

  D20               3                    3     0000    0000    0000    0011
  D21               2                    2     0000    0000    0000    0010
  D22              16                   10     0000    0000    0001    0000
  D23               4                    4     0000    0000    0000    0100
  D24               0                    0     0000    0000    0000    0000
  D25               0                    0     0000    0000    0000    0000
  D30               8                    8     0000    0000    0000    0000
  K2Y0              8                    8                     0000    1000
  T0             0/300
```

Analysis of results

From the monitor details, the following can be determined:

1. The binary value in K2Y0 shows that bit 8 is at logic 1.
2. This corresponds to Y3 being ON.
3. This is correct since the output Y3 was ON when the monitor results were taken.
4. The contents of the stack are shown in the diagram below.

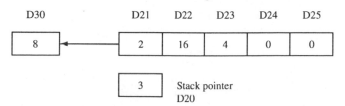

5. This shows the following:

   (a) The contents of D30 = 8, that is the logical value for the output Y3.
   (b) The stack pointer = 3, indicating there are three values left on the stack.
   (c) The values remaining on the stack correspond to the Y Outputs, which have as yet not been used.

Y1	Y4	Y2
2	16	4

20
Assignments

The assessment of BTEC units now requires that a large proportion of the assessment use meaningful assignments. For engineering courses, this requires assignments to be based on carefully thought out industrial applications and scenarios.

With this in mind, it is hoped that the following examples can be used by lecturers and tutors in further and higher education to produce meaningful and stimulating assignments for their students.

For those in engineering who are not using this book as part of an engineering course, it is hoped that they can find the time to try and produce effective solutions.

Nothing can best prepare someone to produce good working PLC programs than 'having a go' themselves once they have acquired the basic skills and knowledge, which it is hoped this book has provided.

1. Modify TRAF1 (page 67) so that traffic lights can automatically control the single-line flow of traffic on a section of road which has one lane closed owing to roadworks.
2. Modify INTLK1 (page 72), so that it could be used in a quiz in which the first contestant who wishes to answer the question can press their button and bring on just their output light. The other contestants' outputs will be inhibited, until a reset button is operated.
3. Modify the PLC sequence controller PNEU2, so that it can operate automatically for 10 complete cycles.
4. Modify CENTRE1 (page 193), so that an alarm will sound if the length of the bar exceeds 500 cm.
5. A stepper motor is driven by 1 second pulses from the output Y0. Each time a pulse is applied to the motor, it rotates by 7.5°. The number of pulses which are to be applied to the motor is obtained from the input switches X0–X7.

   If X0–X7 = 0000 0001, then one pulse is applied to the stepper motor.
   If X0–X7 = 1111 1111, then 255 pulses are applied to the motor.

6. Produce a ladder diagram so that when an 8 bit number from 1 to 255 is input from X0–X7 it will then be divided using a value from 1 to 15, which is input from X10–X13. Let the division part of the program be done using a sub-routine. The answer is then output via Y0 to Y17, to an accuracy of 1 decimal point. That is,

Hundreds	Y17–Y14
Tens	Y13–Y10
Units	Y7–Y4
Tenths	Y3–Y0.

Note

This can be done without using the floating point arithmetic instructions which are now available on version 3.3 FX PLCs.

7. A mail order company has to sort customer deliveries according to the region where they are to be sent (i.e. North, Midlands, South). The packages travel along a conveyor system, where they are scanned by a bar-code reader. Based on the bar-code reading, one of three output solenoids will be energized, to push the package into the correct bin.

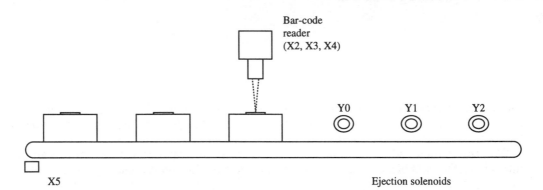

Use three inputs to simulate the bar-code reader and a fourth input, connected to a push button, to simulate the movement of the conveyor.

For the sake of simplicity assume that the packages are all of the same length and that the operation of the push button X5, simulating the movement of the conveyor, is equivalent to the conveyor moving the length of one of the packages.

Let

$$X0 = start$$
$$X1 = stop$$

Bar-code simulator:

X2 = North
X3 = Midlands
X4 = South

Conveyor movement simulator:

X5

Ejection solenoids:

Y0 = North
Y1 = Midlands
Y2 = South

8. The sequential operation of a process plant is obtained by the angular position of the main drive shaft. The position of the shaft is obtained from an attached four-track encoding disk, which uses the Gray code. This is a coding pattern in which only 1 bit changes from one position to the next.

Photo-electric devices are used to obtain the electrical output signals from the encoding disk unit and the use of the Gray code ensures that any slight misalignments in the positioning of the photo-electric cells can only cause a maximum error of one place in the position of the shaft.

It is necessary to decode from Gray code to pure binary to determine what process operation is to be carried out next. The conversion process can be done using digital logic half-adder circuits, but since a PLC is already being used, it would be economical if the conversion could be done using a PLC program instead.

Simulate the encoder disk position, using the inputs X0–X3, and display the converted true binary on the outputs Y0–Y3.

Shaft position	Gray code input				Binary output			
	X3	X2	X1	X0	Y3	Y2	Y1	Y0
0	0	0	0	0	0	0	0	0
1	0	0	0	1	0	0	0	1
2	0	0	1	1	0	0	1	0
3	0	0	1	0	0	0	1	1
4	0	1	1	0	0	1	0	0
5	0	1	1	1	0	1	0	1
6	0	1	0	1	0	1	1	0
7	0	1	0	0	0	1	1	1
8	1	1	0	0	1	0	0	0
9	1	1	0	1	1	0	0	1
10	1	1	1	1	1	0	1	0
11	1	1	1	0	1	0	1	1
12	1	0	1	0	1	1	0	0
13	1	0	1	1	1	1	0	1
14	1	0	0	1	1	1	1	0
15	1	0	0	0	1	1	1	1

4 Bit Gray-Coded Disk

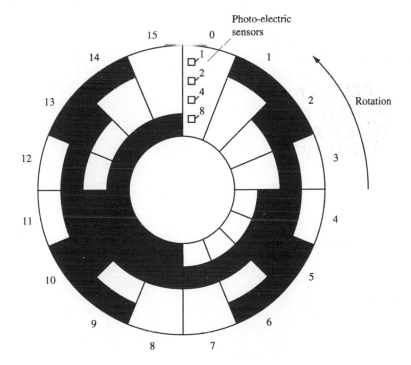

9. Within a bakery, the dough has to be mixed for different lengths of time dependent on the required texture for the finished loaf.
   Modify Delay3 (see page 165) so that the operator can:

   (a) Set up the mixing time within the range 10–20 s.
   (b) On operating the start button, the output Y0 will be immediately energized for the necessary mixing time.
   (c) The timer values cannot be changed while the mixer is on.

10. Produce an accurate 24 hour clock on the Y0–Y17 inputs, that is:

    Y0–Y7   minutes
    Y10–Y17 hours

    Use the inputs X0–X7 to enable the current time to be set into the PLC and use the input X10 to start the clock.

Index